Town and Country
Autumn
Trees

Irene Finch

Longman

Words you may not know

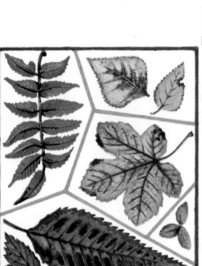

antidotes will stop poisons from causing harm
bast is the inner layer of the bark
bevelled edges always slope away gradually
botanists study plants
branch wrinkles are folds at the base of the branch
burrs can cling with tiny hooks
chinese beards are long branch wrinkles
conifers are trees with cones, like fir cones
coppiced trees are cut off short and then sprout out
cuttings are cut branches that grow roots
deciduous trees lose their leaves in autumn
detergents are used to wash clothes and dishes
embryo plants have not yet grown into proper plants
end-grain wood is cut across the grain
fishbone mosaics have leaves in rows on each side of a branch
fissured bark is split
flexible things bend easily
fluted trunks have deep smooth grooves running down
girdle scars go all round the twig. They are left when bud
    scales fall off in spring
heart wood is dark wood in the centre
honey guides help the bee to find the centre of the flower
hybrid seeds grow on a plant when the flowers are dusted
    with pollen from a slightly different kind of plant. Hybrid
    seeds grow into hybrid plants
infertile seeds will not grow
kilns are containers in which walnuts can be heated and dried
lattices are networks
layered branches are pulled down to the ground and
    fastened, so that new roots can grow
lenticels are small porous patches on twigs and bark
lobes are rounded outgrowths
mites are tiny creatures with eight legs
parasites feed on plants and animals that are still alive
pollarded trees have the branches cut off to leave just a
    trunk. They sprout from the top
predators kill and eat live creatures
pupate: to turn into a resting stage (pupa) before the wings
    are developed
rays in wood are narrow bands that run across
seals are rings of bark that grow over a wound on a tree
    trunk
stunted leaves have not grown full size
sucker shoots grow up from the roots of some trees
turbulent air is full of little currents
variegated leaves have pale patches
weevils are beetles with snouts
whorls of branches grow in rings as shown on page 45

Contents

Collecting and arranging leaves 4
Leaf rubbings 5
Stencils and vein patterns 6
Big leaves 7
Prints 8
Plaster casts 9
Leaf sizes and reference collections 10
Histograms and street maps 11
Maps and models 12
How leaves change colour 13
Colour change and leaf fall 16
Evergreens leaf stalks and leaf scars 17
Buds, fallen leaves 18
Fruits and seeds 20
Winged fruits 21
Fluffy fruits 23
Juicy fruits 24
Cases with seeds inside 27
Nuts 28
Seeds 29
Books 31
How to find the names of your leaves 32
Index 79

Leaf pictures

Damaged leaves 34–35
Leaves with leaflets 38–43
Almost smooth leaves 46–55
Leaves with small teeth only 58–67
Leaves with some big teeth or lobes 70–79

Contents of Growing Trees

Buds in spring
Girdle scars
Leaves
Things that fall from trees
Stems growing
Twigs and trees

Flowers
Seedlings
Bark
Wood
Under the trees
Where trees grow

companion volume to this book

Collecting and arranging leaves

Autumn is the best time for collecting leaves. If you live in a town it may be the only time, for picking is not usually allowed in parks. The autumn leaves have lovely colours and they are tougher than spring leaves, so they keep better. Find as many different kinds as you can, and wash them if necessary.

You can arrange leaves and other finds on a big white plate or a tray lined with paper, pouring on a little water. Or you can make shapes round the leaves and then paint the result, as shown on page 2.

It is a good idea to sort out your leaves. If one group sorts theirs according to colours, and others according to shapes or sizes, you will be able to see the different kinds of sets. At the back of this book there are pages of leaf photographs and they are sorted out in still another way. You will find a list of these sets on page 32. See if you can understand this method of sorting, and try it out on your leaves.

Artists often use the shapes of leaves for making decorations. If you look through the next few pages of this book you will find some ways of doing this. Some methods show up the shape, others show up the veins. Some methods make an accurate picture, but others will give you unusual results and patterns. Most of the methods work best with very flat leaves, which grow in the shade, but plaster casts are often better if the leaf is wavy.

Your prints and stencils can be used to make special wrapping paper, or they can be arranged into a large pattern or picture. They might even make birds or fish or strange plants and men. After all, we are all really made from plant food!

It is hard to paint the shine on a real leaf, and you can make leaf pictures by cutting out materials like satin or shiny paper. Often the underside will need something different, and veins can be stitched on.

Try your first leaf rubbing with a rather thick flat leaf, and put it in a folded piece of paper. Later you can try smaller leaves and single sheets of paper.

Leaf rubbings

Get a soft pencil with a blunt point, or a thick, hard, wax crayon, or, best of all, a piece of heel-ball (from the shoe mender). Rub the paper evenly all over with this, starting on one side and moving steadily across, with no spaces between the streaks. Keep the paper still with the fingers of one hand while you crayon with the other. When you have to move your fingers, try not to lift them all off the paper at once, or the leaf will shift, and spoil your rubbing. Is it better to rub across the main vein or along it? Should the stalk be left on?

Try leaves with the veiny side up and the smooth side up, thick leaves and thin leaves. Usually there is a messy piece of crayoning beyond the edge of the leaf. Try out different ways of dealing with this. You can make your crayon strokes go right to the paper's edge, or cut them off evenly with scissors. If you use tracing paper, you can make your crayon strokes go just as far as the leaf edge, and no further. Or you can cut away the messy part fairly close to the leaf shape, and stick the tidy piece on to paper of the same colour.

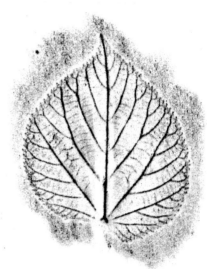

Try dark paper and pale crayons, rough and smooth paper, tissue paper, and different colours. Then try rubbing with an ordinary whitish candle. It will not show, at first, but if you flood dark, watery paint over the whole paper, without scrubbing it, the pattern will come up. This is called the 'wax-resist' method, and it works better on some kinds of paper than others.

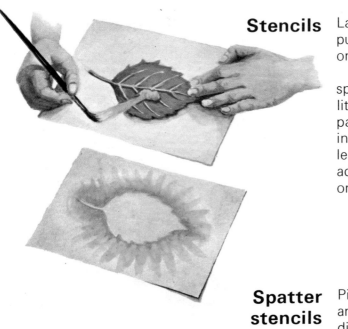

Stencils

Lay a flat leaf on clean paper, then put a small pile of powder paint on the leaf.

Use your finger, a piece of dry sponge, or a dry brush, to push a little paint outwards on to the paper. Do this all the way round in a star shape, then lift off the leaf. Try using damp paper or adding other colours as you go, or dabbing with a damp sponge.

Spatter stencils

Pin a leaf on to a newspaper pad, and then hold a tooth brush, dipped in wet paint, above it. Rub under the bristles with a stiff stick (it is best to wear an overall). Try to get small spatter drops, close together. If the space looks too bare when the leaf is unpinned, spatter it a little.

Vein patterns

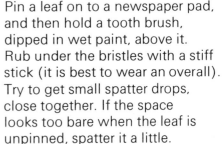

On page 31 there are some leaves with different vein patterns. They have been used to make a design for a book cover. Look through your leaves for interesting vein patterns, holding the dark ones up to the light. You can show vein patterns by painting, prints or embroidery. Or you can try pins, pushed hard into a cork mat, and wound twice with cotton.

Which leaf is bigger? The bottom one is longer but it may not be bigger in area. The top one is wider, but it is made partly of big teeth, and the dents between the teeth do not count in the area.

Big leaves

To find the area of a leaf, make a stencil on squared paper and count the squares.

To find a really big leaf, look at small plants in sheltered places as well as trees. Big leaves are more easily torn by high winds. If a big leaf is divided into leaflets it may let the wind through without tearing. But leaflets are very deceiving and may not be as big as you think.

If you press a large leaf after the stencil is made, you will see if it shrinks as it dries. It may not quite fit. To stop this drying and shrinking, try wax polish. It works for a time because it is waterproof. It can also stop leaves from curling up. Evergreen leaves have their own wax and may not shrink much.

Of course, the leaf with the biggest area may not be the heaviest or the thickest.

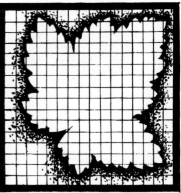

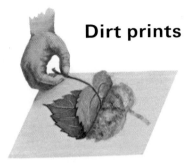

Dirt prints

Ordinary leaves at the end of the year can get very dirty, especially in towns. Make a piece of paper damp by painting or dripping water over it, lay on a dirty leaf, dirty side down, then put another piece of paper on top. Rub well, and see if you can get a print. Does soapy water help?

Paint-and-detergent prints

Make a thick mixture of any kind of dark paint, and add a drop of washing-up liquid, Gloy, or glycerine to help it spread nicely without too many bubbles. Put a little of the mixture on a brush, and spread it *thinly* over a fresh leaf. It is usually best to lay the leaf on newspaper while you do this. Then squeeze out your brush and mop off all blobs of paint from the leaf.

Now lay the painted leaf on clean paper, paint side down. Place a piece of card or paper on top, and rub gently all over. Try a second print, without adding more paint, and then try painting the veiny side and the smooth side, to compare them. Mix suitable colours carefully, not necessarily the colours of the real leaf. More than one colour can be used on the same leaf, and some prints look better if they overlap. Prints can also be made from slices of fruits.

Lino printing paint is very good for this work, and the roller and glass plate can be used just as for a lino-cut. An office ink pad can also be used, but there are not many colours.

Plaster casts

To make these you will need Plasticine, an old basin and spoon, some good quality plaster of Paris and a plastic sheet to work on. If you want straight edges to the plaster cast, find some straight pieces of wood.

Flatten some Plasticine on your base-sheet and vaseline it *slightly*. Then lay a *small thick* leaf on it and press it in, either with your fingers or by rolling a pencil over. If the leaf is not flat, mould the Plasticine roughly to fit it, then press on the leaf to get the final shape.

Now pull off the leaf and build a Plasticine wall or a vaselined wooden wall round the print. The leaf impression is now at the bottom of a *mould*.

Mix a *little* plaster with water till it is just runny. Pour it quickly into the mould: you must not wait about. Leave it to set: you can feel it get hot. But wash up the spoon and basin immediately, making sure you do not block the sink. If you do not wash up at once, the plaster will set and cannot be liquefied again. If there was not enough plaster, make a little more and pour on top. Cheap quality plaster should be left several hours to set, but if the mould was small you can pull it off good plaster after about half an hour.

Later try larger leaves, or mixing paint with the plaster before you pour. If the leaf has no small teeth, try building the Plasticine wall right against the leaf outline.

A large mould can have several prints arranged on it, and can be strengthened with wire. Perhaps you can think of other things to use than leaves. Try rolling a soaked fir cone or a knobbly twig across the Plasticine.

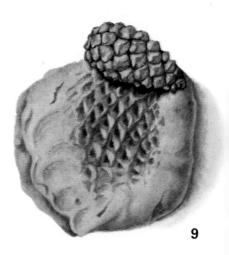

9

Leaf sizes and shapes

Try to find leaves of different sizes that have fallen from the same tree, and see which are the biggest and the smallest. Look at them carefully to see if there are different shapes as well as sizes.

Then mark out a little patch of ground with about 50 leaves on it, all fallen from the same tree, and pick up *every single leaf* on that patch, not just the nice ones. When you get back, sort the leaves into sizes. You could have one pile of leaves from 1 to 2 cm. wide, the next 2 to 3 cm., and so on. Lay out the piles in order, and label them. Usually there are bulging piles in the middle. You can see from this which are the commonest sizes and which are the rarest. If you count the numbers in each pile you can make a diagram like this (a histogram). Remember the shape of this histogram, for you may find it again, when you measure the sizes and weights of other things, or even of boys and girls in a class. The rarest sizes are the biggest and the smallest, but the bulge will not be in the same place every time. If you collect fallen plane leaves in different months, the position of the bulge moves along.

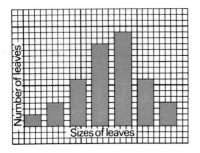

Naming leaves and making labelled collections

When you have looked at the shape and the veins of your leaves, you can find the names, using page 32. Then each leaf or print can be labelled, to help other people.

To press leaves, put them between thick newspaper in a dry place, with a good pile of books on top, till they are quite dry. Change the paper on the second day or whenever it feels damp. The finished leaves can be stuck on paper with a rubbery glue or with strips of sticky paper (*not* Sellotape). Store them in a box.

Transparent adhesive plastic makes a good covering for *fresh* leaves but is not cheap. Find a stiff card, and cut the plastic slightly bigger. Peel the backing off the plastic and lay the leaf on the sticky side. Then place the card on top and fold in the edges. These cards should be pressed with books till the leaf is dry, but then they can be stored like a card index.

Here is a histogram, made on squared paper, to show the commonest trees in a street. There were 20 lime trees, so the column for lime is 20 squares high. The histogram shows also the number of plane trees, and the name of the rarest tree. Hedges are difficult unless you start off by counting the number of *houses* that have lime, privet, etc. Would this give the same kind of histogram? You can make histograms of a wood or a park, as well as a street.

Counts and histograms

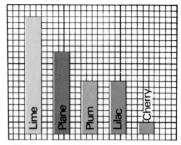

This is a side-view of the front gardens in a street (called an *elevation*). The distances between trees were measured by pacing them out with a practised two-foot stride. Then they were drawn on paper, allowing one centimetre for every 10 feet. The heights of the trees were not measured, but estimated. The drawing below is a *plan* of the same street, as seen from above. You can trace out the same trees in plan and elevation. A hedge can be mapped in the same way.

Strip maps

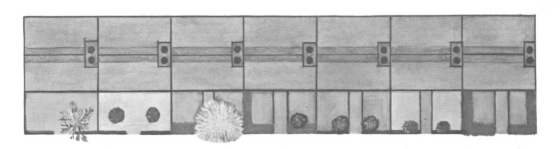

If you can find a street map of your district, try to mark on it the positions of rare or interesting trees, so that others can find them.

Street maps

Mapping trees in the park

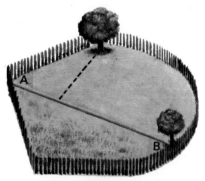

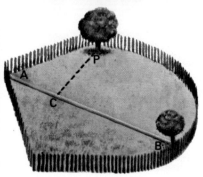

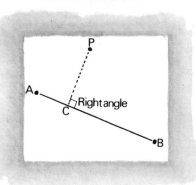

It is best to ask permission first, from the park-keeper.

1. Make a rough plan of the park on paper, showing the paths and trees. Choose only *part* of a big park, or divide the work out.

2. Rule a straight pencil line AB across your rough plan. Then make the same straight line AB across the real park, with rope (or a line of sticks). Lie on the ground and sight along the rope to check that it is straight. You may need something to lie on.

3. Choose your first tree and mark it 'P' on the rough plan.

4. Walk along the rope line AB till the chosen tree P is exactly opposite you. The spot where you are standing has been marked 'C' in this drawing. When you stand here, if you are really opposite the tree P, then your sighting line CP should be exactly at right angles to the rope AB. Check whether this is so by using a big wooden or card right-angle, laying it on the ground and sighting along it. If it is not a right-angle, move yourself a little further along and keep trying till you find the right spot.

5. Then measure the distance from A to C and from C to P. Write these down, with the name of the tree.

6. Make measurements, of the same kind, for other trees and for corners of fences, crossings of paths, etc., either now or later.

7. For the accurate plan, draw the line AB on a fresh piece of paper, to scale. One centimetre can represent ten feet.

8. Draw in AC to the same scale. Then make a right-angle at C and measure off CP. Label the tree. Put in other measured points and finish off the paths and fences.

Models

A plan of the park can turn into a model if you stick it on a flat board and make model trees. You can use twigs, electric flex, coloured sponge or sawdust, bits of plants or anything suitable. Try to find something to make paths, grass and fences, but use strong glue, or your work will be wasted.

There are different ways of changing colour.
See what you can find.

Changing evenly to yellow, then brown.

Starting at the edge and moving in.

Veins turning brown first.

Starting between the veins

Leaving patches between the veins.

Starting in irregular spots.

These trees have red and yellow colours all the year.

The oldest leaves may change first, or the smallest.

Some trees have two ways of changing

Red or purple leaves may turn orange.

Some leaves turn red, then orange, where the sunlight falls, but not where they have been shaded.

A big tree may change sooner than a pruned one.

Some kinds of tree always change early, some are evergreen.

A tree in a dry place, or one part of a tree, may change early.

Leaves often stay green round an injury or a gall.

Colour change and leaf fall

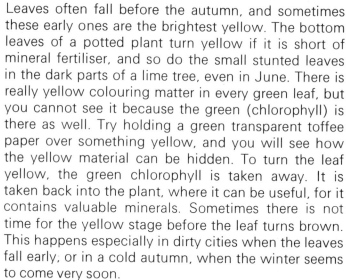

Leaves often fall before the autumn, and sometimes these early ones are the brightest yellow. The bottom leaves of a potted plant turn yellow if it is short of mineral fertiliser, and so do the small stunted leaves in the dark parts of a lime tree, even in June. There is really yellow colouring matter in every green leaf, but you cannot see it because the green (chlorophyll) is there as well. Try holding a green transparent toffee paper over something yellow, and you will see how the yellow material can be hidden. To turn the leaf yellow, the green chlorophyll is taken away. It is taken back into the plant, where it can be useful, for it contains valuable minerals. Sometimes there is not time for the yellow stage before the leaf turns brown. This happens especially in dirty cities when the leaves fall early, or in a cold autumn, when the winter seems to come very soon.

In the end, most leaves turn brown if the air and water can get at them, but they sometimes keep their colour quite well under adhesive plastic. The yellow chemicals are then not destroyed. Try out different ways of keeping or changing the colour.

A few trees turn red in autumn, and this is because they make a new red colouring material. Sunlight and cold nights help this red chemical to form, but we do not know its use: perhaps it has none. Some plants can never make the red colouring. Other plants, like copper beech and red cabbage, make plenty all the year round, and some trees seem to have more in the *young* leaves. Try to find out what will happen if a leaf has red and yellow, or red and green colouring matter, together. It depends partly on the kind and amount of each colour.

Leaves sometimes start falling from the tips of the twigs, sometimes from the bottom. This gives beech and elm trees a different look in autumn.

Evergreens

You are not likely to find holly leaves falling in autumn, for holly is an evergreen. Evergreens are popular in town parks, so see how many different kinds you can find. Are the leaves different from those of other trees? And do they ever fall? Privet is usually called evergreen, but look at the privet bushes in your neighbourhood through the autumn and winter and see if they do keep all their leaves.

Leaf stalks

Most leaves have stalks, but some are long, some short, and some trees have both kinds. Poplar leaf stalks are flat, but some trees have cylindrical stalks, others, gutter-shaped, like an arch upside down. Try out these three shapes (cylinder, gutter, and flat) with a strip of paper, and see which shapes are stiff and which are flexible in one direction. A stiff leaf stalk can hold a leaf out to the sun, but a flexible one can give to the winds. Look at the leaves on the trees and see if the stalks make them stiff or fluttery.

The base of the leaf stalk is wide, to make a good join and to protect the side-bud that grows in the angle. Does every leaf have a side-bud? (See page 32.) If you look at the bases of different leaves you will sometimes find small green wings.

Leaf scars

Pull off a leaf that seems ready to come, and look at the scar it makes. It comes off easily because a loose layer was formed across the leaf base and the scar is neat because it is already protected with a layer of cork. Above it, there is a side-bud. Look at other leaf scars and see if they are always the same kind of shape. Some of them have little dots, the veins. Ash, horse-chestnut and the tree of heaven have big leaf scars that are worth seeing, and the plane has a very unusual one. Pull off a plane leaf carefully, to see how this works.

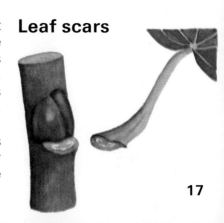

17

Buds

Ash Beech Willow

Oak Lime Sycamore

Tree buds often get dirty in winter, but under the dirt they may be red, brown, green or sooty black. They can also have very different shapes and scales, as you can see from these pictures. Sometimes the buds grow in pairs, but sometimes they are on alternate sides of the stem. Other twigs seem to have rather irregular buds but they are really in a spiral. Some buds stick out from the stem, but others lie close, and at the top there may be a single bud or a cluster.

If you are studying one tree, go through these points and check them. Also look at the colour and thickness of the twigs, and see if there are old fruits or new catkins. Gradually you can learn to recognise trees from the winter twigs, and it may help if you make a dried collection.

Fallen leaves

Dead leaves are made mostly of a material called cellulose, and so are paper, wood, cotton thread and cloth, viscose rayon, and cellulose sponges. Most cellulose alters when it gets wet: dry leaves will crunch under your feet, but not wet ones. Choose one kind of cellulose and try out one or two of these tests. You will find that manufactured cellulose is sometimes different from the natural material.

Compare a thoroughly wet piece and a dry piece. How far will they bend without cracking? Which is stiffer? more brittle? more pliable? Do they stretch, like elastic, when you hang a weight on the end? Do they break with the weight? Do they crease? Why does a properly pressed leaf stay flat? What happens if you soak it? Try ironing a damp tea towel and a dry one.

Tie up a cellulose sponge with string and let it dry out. Then untie it. Try wetting again. Could you fix a leaf into a cylinder shape?

Does a leaf change size when it dries? Keep it pressed flat. Or try drying a cellulose sponge, for size.

Cellulose sponges are less strong than nylon, but they can mop up a lot of water. Try to measure how much water a cellulose sponge will mop out of a jar. Dead leaves can take up so much water that they prevent flooding after heavy rain. When forests are cut down, floods often increase. Try to see how much water a handful of sodden leaves can hold. Weigh them wet, then again after you have dried them out. This water is held even when the leaves are partly decayed, as in peat (bulb fibre) and leaf mould, so these are useful to plants in the garden. When dead leaves finally decay they also give out mineral fertiliser.

Horsechestnut leaves decay fast, but beech leaves only slowly. See what happens to other leaves. Sometimes the veins are left as a skeleton. If you keep some damp leaves in a tin, you may see the little threads of fungus that cause the decay. Some grow little white or coloured heads, with powdery spores that blow off and infect other places. Some have much bigger spore heads, called toadstools. If you lay a toadstool umbrella, right way up, on green paper, and keep it still in a tin, you may see the spore dust by next day. Take care, as some toadstools are poisonous.

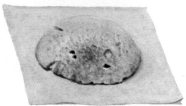

Fruits and seeds

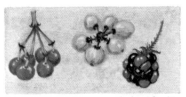

Juicy fruits

Winged fruits and seeds

Fluffy fruits and seeds

Hard cases with large seeds

Hard cases with small seeds inside

Galls with maggots or escape holes

Autumn is the time for most fruits and seeds, but elm, willow and poplar can flower so early that their fruits are ready before this. On the other hand, aucuba and plane are late. Aucuba fruits are not really ripe till autumn is over, and plane fruits usually stay on the tree till the *next* spring. A calendar of fruits would be worth making, to show what is ready when.

Collect a few fruits of all the kinds you can find, and try to sort them out into groups, perhaps the groups in these pictures. Which of your groups has the most kinds? Galls are not fruits at all, but lumps caused by irritation of a pest. If you keep the gall you may breed out the pest. Do not eat fruits or seeds unless you really know they are safe: laburnum and yew seeds are poisonous.

Seeds are usually found inside fruits, like apple pips in an apple. But some fruits, like plums, have only one seed inside. Many seed cases are hard and uneatable, like the pods round pea seeds. A botanist would call these cases 'fruits', when he was botanising, but when he sat down for a meal he would expect 'fruit' to mean something he could eat. In this book, we shall use the word 'fruit' in the botanical meaning.

You can guess that these wings catch the wind and help it to carry the fruits away. This certainly happens, but many fruits have a special kind of wing that can whirl round, keeping almost horizontal, so that the fruit falls *very* slowly. This slow fall is useful, for it gives the wind more time to carry the fruit along. On a windy day, you can try this out with two fruits. Cut the wing off one, but leave it on the other. Drop them both together from a good height, say 8 feet, and see which hits the ground first and which travels further. Try it more than once. You can also try with a handkerchief parachute, and see how much difference it makes to have the 'wing' of cloth horizontal or vertical. This is done by altering the lengths of the strings, as in the drawings, but keeping the same weight hanging from them.

Here are some other ideas you can try out. It is better to pick out one to try properly, and show other people.

If you have found different kinds of winged fruits, see which kinds can do the whirling trick, and which have the slowest fall. A stopwatch is ideal for timing, but you can manage by counting fast and evenly. Sometimes a fruit will whirl on one test, and then delay or fail the next time. Try holding it different ways up, in all the positions you can think of, before letting go. And see how it is held on the tree. Should sycamores be tested in pairs or separated? Do you always get the same result when you try the same fruit, held the same way, several times? If not, you must try averaging, or if the times vary very much, try to think why. If you think the short times are due to something going wrong, you could take the *best* time out of three trials, instead of the *average*.

Are the slow fallers always the lightest? If you cannot weigh one fruit accurately, weight a large number and divide to find the weight of one. The effects of weight can also be tried out with a lime wing that has three or four fruits. Time it with all the fruits on, then remove one at a time.

Fruits with wings

Sycamore

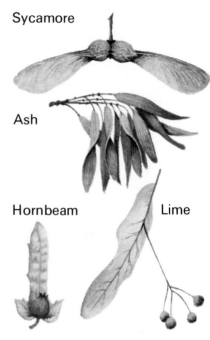

Ash

Hornbeam   Lime

On a windy day you can measure which kinds travel furthest. Do they do better if they start higher up? The wind strength keeps changing, and this could give unfair results. Would it be better to test all the specimens of one kind first, and then the others, or to try them alternately?

Can you estimate the number of sycamore fruits on one tree? You need to find the average number in a bunch, then on a branch, then the number of branches. What happens to them all? Try to see. Why does the tree produce so many?

After a gale, look on the ground round a sycamore tree and see where the fruits fell. There are two ways of counting them. One way is to draw a circle round the tree, with a radius of a yard, and collect all the fruits that travelled less than that. Then draw a two-yard circle, and so on. Another way is to divide the ground out into squares, each a foot across, and count the number of fruits in each square. The numbers can be put on a map. Often the fruits travel more to one side than the other. Check on the things that might cause this. Could it be the wind, other trees or buildings, the slope of the ground, or rough ground catching the fruits?

Most fruits only fall when they are ripe: lime fruits come down in August, but others are much later. There are many good books about the weather that will tell you how to make a wind measuring apparatus or how to use the simpler Beaufort scale. Does a strong wind bring down more fruits? Or is it the rain? Regular records may give you the answer. This means counting all the fruits that fall from your tree each day. If there are too many, divide them into four equal piles, count one pile and multiply by four.

Young trees of ash and sycamore often keep their fruits a long time. Is the wind less lower down? If you make a vane like the one in the diagram, from card, twisted wire and cotton, you can hold it at different heights in the wind.

If you take a ripe birch catkin apart you will find protective leaves and tiny two-winged fruits (left hand drawing). The fruits travel very well (page 57).

Both winged fruits and fluffy fruits use the wind, but very few trees have fluffy fruits, and it is rare to see them in autumn. Willows and poplars (page 57) have little fruit cases that mostly ripen early and give out fluffy seeds. The plane tree has fruits (page 69) that look ripe in autumn but do not come down till next spring. To study fluffy fruits in autumn you can use those from smaller plants, and then compare the tree fruits next year. (Of course the tall trees have an advantage, and you can see how far their seeds travel and find whether the fluff slows their fall, like a wing, or holds water for the seed.)

Try the effect of dripping water on different fluffy fruits, and of shutting them in a tin with a damp cloth. Then dry them out. Look at the fluff with a lens.

Most fluffy fruits grow low down, but winged fruits usually come from high up. Release a winged fruit and a fluffy fruit over a radiator. Wings can slow the fall, like a parachute, but the fluff can actually let the seed rise up in a warm up-current. Find which of the fluffy fruits work best, and which keep steady in the air. Damaged fruits do badly.

Try to find out if there are up-currents like this out of doors, and whether the fluffy fruits can use them. On sunny days there are usually plenty of small up-currents over a playground, but any wind shifts them sideways. If you release a fluffy fruit near the ground, sometimes it will be in a little up-current, and make a hop, but sometimes it will just fall. Some fruits will make several hops, and they may not all be in the same direction. They may even go round in an eddy. This shows that the air near the ground is turbulent, with a lot of small currents in different directions. On windy days the strong sideways movement of the air hides this turbulence. Are the hops as big when the sun is overcast? On a still, sunny day it is sometimes possible to make a big up-current by laying a dry board on a damp lawn. Hot fields and roads, or even big chimneys, can make such big up-currents that they go right up to the cold upper layers of the air and form 'heap' clouds (cumulus) on sunny days. Glider pilots find these up-currents useful, and so do hovering vultures.

Fluffy fruits and seeds

Juicy Fruits

These fruits usually stay on the tree a fair time, so you can find the names from the leaves. Watch how the colour changes as the fruits ripen. Can you see any point in this? Does the inside change at the same time?

Cut open the fruits, but remember that some are poisonous. Check this (see books on page 31), or else treat them all as dangerous, make sure no small children can touch them, and wash your hands carefully.

Some of the seeds inside have a patterned wall, but you need a good achromatic lens to see this. Hold the lens right against your eye and bring the seed near, keeping it in the light. The lens will help you see other things, like the veins on a sycamore fruit, and the wings of a birch fruit. My grandfather used to tell of a rich man who made his living by putting wooden pips in plum jam and selling it for raspberry. Look at a raspberry pip with a lens and see what you think. (Blackberry pips are much the same.)

Some seeds in juicy fruits are covered in a very hard coat, e.g. cherry and plum. Try cracking them open. But some seeds are smaller and have stiff and slippery jelly coats, like those in tomatoes and gooseberries. Look inside all your fruits and make notes, drawings or collections, of the kinds of seeds, and the numbers.

Many fruits are firm enough to cut across cleanly, or slice in layers, either crosswise or lengthwise. Look at the patterns when they are cut, and find good ones. Make drawings or prints with the juice or with paint. Try to work out the different parts that make up the pattern. Sometimes you cut across seeds and their little stalks. Sometimes there are layers of different colours. Sometimes there are veins that change their position in different cuts, and the whole shape and size may change, too. Many fruits have little compartments for the seeds, but the numbers vary. You can use shop fruit as well as wild kinds.

Some holly and aucuba bushes have flowers but no fruit. You will find the reason if you look at the flowers, next year.

Will birds eat any of your fruits? Which do they prefer? Try them on a bird table, but also watch the bushes where these fruits grow, and see when the birds eat them, and which birds. Sometimes, fruits seem to be left until bad weather comes along, or even until next spring. Do you see birds eating poisonous berries? Some animals seem able to eat berries or toadstools that would poison us. Rabbits have an antidote to one toadstool poison in their stomachs.

The bush seems almost to invite the birds to eat its fruits, but what will happen then to the seeds inside? Bears and mice also eat fruits, and so do we. The seeds sometimes pass right through the animal's digestive system, and will then fall to the ground in its droppings. They will be far from the place where they grew and supplied with a little manure. Some seeds survive being chewed, or ground in the birds gizzard and attacked by digestive juices. The jelly coats and stony coats of the seeds may help. You can check on this by trying to grow seeds from birds' droppings, but you may have to keep them through the winter, and the way to do this is described on page 30. You scrape up the droppings with an old spoon, but do not plant them in ordinary soil, for there may be seeds in it already. You will have to grow them on something that cannot have seeds in, or else boil or bake the soil well before you use it. One way is to use a square pickle bottle, with a lid, and a piece of wet plastic sponge inside.

Some seeds certainly seem to travel like this, e.g. the blackberry plant in this blocked gutter.

Look for other fruits growing high up, where birds perch. Some juicy fruits have such hard stones that the seeds cannot grow out easily unless they have been softened by digestion. If you try growing seeds from your fruits, it may help to rub them with a file.

Some seeds of juicy fruits are not swallowed. Pigeons have a small gullet for cherry stones, and cough them up from the crop. Birds are supposed to cough up rose seeds because of the hairs round them. Many birds cough up indigestible matter in *pellets*. Owls have pellets of mouse bones, etc., but robins have pellets containing insect remains. Some berries colour the birds' pellets. Look out for this on fences near elderberry bushes. And *we* spit out cherry stones, so you can find cherry seedlings growing along many town streets, and apple seedlings from discarded cores.

Mistletoe grows on trees, and it has fleshy fruits with a sticky juice. See if the birds like them. Many do, but the sticky seeds are often cleaned from their beaks by wiping against a tree branch. Can you see the point of this?

We eat many wild fruits that seem the same as those of the Stone Age, and must have been eaten by our ancestors. But many wild fruits are small and sour, like wild apples and plums. The modern improved varieties were gradually developed from them. All plants grown from seed vary a bit, and somebody hit on the idea of *selecting* only the best to grow. In time, the modern varieties were produced, some of them by using pollen from plants found abroad. This work takes great patience, for many poor plants are produced for every good one. When a good one is produced, e.g., the Cox's Orange apple, grown by Mr. Cox from a pip, it will not usually grow 'true' from seed, and is multiplied by budding and grafting, which are described in gardening books.

Many of our fruits were brought in from abroad, starting with the Romans. Many came from America when that continent was discovered, and others from China. Try to find out the origin of the trees you study.

These do not fall off the trees quickly, so you can name them by their leaves. Some of the cases have unusual shapes. You need sharp eyes to find some of them, like Buddleia and lilac, which are often missed.

Try to open some of the cases and find the seeds. Some may be very hard and need soaking. Some open of themselves, if you let them dry. The horsechestnut has a case that often opens as soon as it falls to the ground, and it has a very few, large seeds inside, the conkers. Pine cones do not have a proper case, and they will open out on their own if they are ripe and you keep them dry. Then you can try wetting them again. When there is a proper case, it may be divided into compartments and there may be few or many seeds inside. Then look at the seeds. Some are plain, but some are fluffy and some have wings. When you finally sort out all your seeds and fruits, it is usually best to put the winged seeds with the winged fruits.

A special warning is needed about laburnum seeds. They are very poisonous and could kill small children, so it is best not to put them in an open collection.

These cases protect the seeds very well, but some of them have an extra use. Broom and gorse have a case that explodes and shoots out the seeds when they get dry. Look at the exploded ones and you will see the two halves of the case are strongly twisted. In the unopened case the two halves are joined along their edges and cannot twist. As they dry, they pull on the seams, and finally split open violently, shooting the seeds out. Pick some with stalks and stand them in a jar in the middle of a table, leaving them to dry, to see what happens. They are related to peas, and the valves of a pea pod also twist as they dry, but the cultivated peas are too big to be shot out. Laburnum pods also twist open, but not very well, and they do not shoot far.

Hard cases with small seeds inside

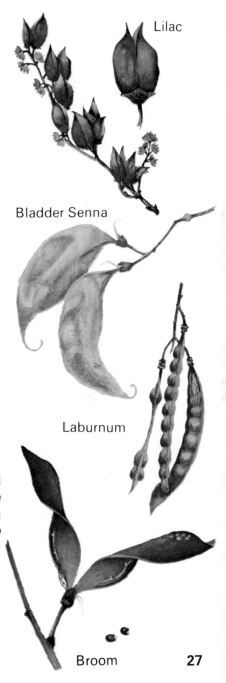

Lilac

Bladder Senna

Laburnum

Broom

Nuts

Sweet Chestnut

Acorn

Try opening some of the other big fruits, like acorns and sweet chestnuts. Usually these have only one seed inside, so they are called *nuts*. Some cases are so tough that they need soaking, boiling or cracking. Acorns have an extra protection outside the fruit: the cup (or cupule). Beech and sweet chestnut have this cupule so enlarged that it covers the fruits themselves, opening when they are ripe. You may have to work quite hard to get down to the beech or sweet chestnut seed. First there is the cupule to take off, then the tough brown fruit case. Inside that there is a thin brown seed coat, and then the big seed itself. Nuts can be bought at the shop if none grow near you. Hazel nuts often still have a cupule.

Ripe nuts fall straight down under the tree and it is hard to be sure how they travel to new places. Pigeons, jays and squirrels take acorns, but do they eat them all up? Have you ever found an oak seedling far from an oak tree? Some birds take nuts. Mice and voles come by night and also eat a great many. So do the squirrels. And sometimes, when you open a nut, you will find an insect grub eating it. When these grubs are fully fed they turn into moths or flies or into the long-snouted beetles called weevils. We like to eat some of these nuts, but acorns would make you ill, and people only used to eat them after special cooking. Even pigs can manage only a few without harm. Sweet chestnuts are particularly good when cooked, but they do not grow well in our climate.

Beech and some other trees have very few nuts in most years and then suddenly have a 'mast' year, with an enormous crop, after a good summer. Botanists have suggested that if there is a glut in one year, the mice cannot destroy the lot, but if the supply was evenly spread out, the mice could multiply and keep up with it, and not a seedling would be left.

Seeds

You will almost always find seeds in a fruit, like peas in a pod. A seed has a seed coat and then a little plant inside it, curled up and waiting to grow. It is only half developed, so it is called an *embryo* plant. But most seeds already have a small root and two peculiar fat leaves, swollen up with food. In between these seed leaves is a very small bud.

Sycamore seeds may be easier to open if they are slightly dry and limp inside. First you open the fruit and find it has a furry lining. The seed inside is in a reddish brown seed case. Peel it off and you will find the little sycamore embryo inside, coiled up. Uncoil it carefully and you will find the two green seed-leaves joined to a very small root. Between the leaves is a very tiny bud.

If you open an ash fruit you will find the seed in its seed case but the embryo is hard to make out for it is buried in a mass of food. Look for other seeds that are big enough to open. If they are in a fruit case, get them out of this first. Peel off the hard case of an acorn or beech nut and you will find the thin seed coat. Try a sweet chestnut, or a walnut, which will need careful cracking, or a hazel nut. Avoid nuts that have been kiln-dried, as they are too brittle. You need fresh ones. Some *very* fresh ones are brittle, too, but if you leave them in the air after taking off the fruit wall, they will lose a little moisture and become flexible. The bulk of the nut is made of the seed leaves but they may be very large and twisted. If you can separate them gently, and find where they join together, that will show you where to look for the root. Sometimes you can see the root sticking out at one end.

Sycamore

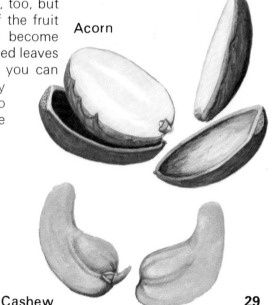

Acorn

Cashew

29

The food in seeds

The seed has a store of food in it to help the new plant to grow. Most have starchy food, that turns black with a dab of iodine. Some seeds have fat in them, too, and all have protein, the body-building food. We eat the food store of seeds such as peas, wheat, and nuts.

Keeping the seeds over the winter

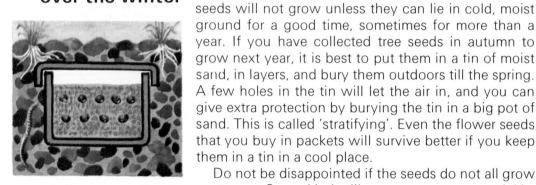

During the winter most seeds lie in the ground and many are eaten or attacked by moulds. But most tree seeds will not grow unless they can lie in cold, moist ground for a good time, sometimes for more than a year. If you have collected tree seeds in autumn to grow next year, it is best to put them in a tin of moist sand, in layers, and bury them outdoors till the spring. A few holes in the tin will let the air in, and you can give extra protection by burying the tin in a big pot of sand. This is called 'stratifying'. Even the flower seeds that you buy in packets will survive better if you keep them in a tin in a cool place.

Do not be disappointed if the seeds do not all grow next year. Some kinds, like sycamore, grow quickly, but others take more than a year to sprout. Seeds that fall in summer should be planted straight away.

Large seeds and small seeds

Do bigger trees have bigger seeds?

A horsechestnut seed probably weighs a thousand times as much as a birch seed. Which is better? If a tree has big seeds it may have fewer: compare different trees and see what you think. The big seed usually falls to the ground nearby, and cannot travel far. But it has a good store of food inside it, to give it a really good start in life, and it can survive a long time in places where the light is dim, amongst grass or under other trees.

A little seed like the birch has such a tiny food store that it can only grow a very little with its own food supplies, without light. If it falls even among grass, it has not the strength to grow above it, as an acorn could, so it will die. The only birch seeds that can live are those that fall on bare soil or in moss, in the open. But birch trees can produce so many of these tiny seeds, and they are so light, that they blow everywhere and are very likely to find almost every suitable spot.

Books

There are many good books in libraries that will help you with trees, and there is not room to write them all on this page. Look on the shelves for two Dewey numbers: 582.16, which is the Plants section, and 634.9, which is Forestry. Sometimes there are more books under 635.9, which is Gardening.

M. E. Selsam, *Things to do with Trees*, Chatto and Windus.

E. Johnson, *Seven Trees*, Blackwell.

S. A. Manning, *Trees and Forests*, Blackwell.

S. R. Badmin, *Trees in Britain*, Pelican.

C. A. Hall, *British Trees*, Black.

G. E. Hyde, *Trees*, E. J. Arnold.
    Wild Fruits, E. J. Arnold.

P. Chadwick, *Trees in Fruit*, Cassell.

W. P. Westell and K. Harvey, *Trees*, Macmillan.

J. Pokovny, *Trees of Parks and Gardens*, Spring Books.

B. Taylor, *Timber*, Univ. of London Press.

N. Wymer, *Timber*, John Baker.

J. Hornby, *Forestry in Britain*, Macmillan.

D. H. Chapman, *Seasons and the Woodman*, O.U.P.

M. Hadfield, *Your Book of Trees*, Faber.

Harder books with special uses

E. Kiaer, *Garden Trees and Shrubs*, Blandford, coloured pictures.

Woodland Life, Ed. A. Darlington, Blandford, pictures of galls.

A. G. L. Hellyer, *Shrubs in Colour*, very good coloured pictures, expensive, Collingridge.

A. M. Coats, *Garden Shrubs and their Histories*, Vista, explorers, origins of names, etc.

P. Edwards, *Trees and the British Landscape*, Bell, history of forests and parks.

Poisonous Plants, H.M.S.O., reliable information about poisonous plants.

Vedel, Helge and Lange, *Trees and Bushes in Wood and Hedgerow*, Methuen, very good coloured pictures of trees and a history of forests since the Ice Ages.

H. L. Edlin, *Wayside and Woodland Trees*, Warne, good pictures, keys to leaves and twigs, information about the history and uses of trees.

R. Gurney, *Trees of Britain*, Faber, details of structure and drawings of seedlings.

Finding the name of your tree.

The leaves on one tree are not all the same, so decide first which is the commonest shape and size of leaf, and use that. The colours do not matter: they are variations that will have the same name as the green leaves.

Then try to decide if you have leaves or leaflets. When the leaf is still on the tree, this is easy. If you have several small leaves on a stem, each one has a little bud where the leaf joins on.

If you have a single leaf with leaflets, there is only one bud, where the real leaf joins the main stem. Leaflets never have buds of their own.

But in autumn, many trees cast their leaflets *separately*, and after they have fallen it is difficult to tell what they are. Try looking at the tree for any leaves that are still whole, or look for the midribs or stalks, which may be lying on the ground.

The pages of photographs are in sets. Here is a list of the sets.

Damaged leaves: 34, 35
Leaves with leaflets: 38–43
Leaves without leaflets:
    smooth or nearly smooth outline
    (some are needles) 46–55
    small teeth only 58–67
    large teeth or large rounded lobes
    (often small teeth also) 70–78

If you cannot decide between two sets, look at both. Look at *every photograph in the set,* checking the shape, texture and veins, and whether there are wings on the stalk. Remember that sizes of leaves can vary, and try to check the points that have been printed *behind* the picture page. You will also see some ideas there, for the whole year.

If you cannot find your trees in *this* book, try some of those on page 31, both for wild and for cultivated trees. If this fails, ask the park-keeper or your local Natural History Society for help.

Leaf miners
These are small grubs living protected between the two skins of the leaf, and eating the soft green part inside. Hold the leaf up to the light, or open it, and you will see the two skins, the droppings and perhaps the grub. One end of the mine is narrower and perhaps you can think why. If you keep the leaf healthy, the grub will probably pupate in the mine, and then you may see what kind of adult is formed: fly, weevil, moth or sawfly.

Frosts, wind and poor light
Young leaves battered against branches will have splits and brown marks, or frost can make them crumple. Older leaves may wither at the edges in frosty weather, or they may go limp, but sometimes recover later on. Very poor light seems to stop leaves from growing full size, but slight shade and severe pruning can make them grow very big and flat. Tiny brown spots on leaves or fruit may be caused by a sucking insect or by a fungus.

Leaf damage and native trees
It is interesting to check your leaves for damage, and see which is the commonest kind of damage in your neighbourhood. Which trees have the biggest proportion of damaged leaves? Do evergreens suffer less? Do British trees have more pests than trees that have been brought in from abroad? Perhaps the pests get left behind. If you like birds you will find that bluetits and other insect-eaters are attracted to trees that have insect pests, but gardeners are not!

It is often difficult to find out if a plant is really native to Britain, and the distinction is not always a definite one. Before the Great Ice Ages, we had many trees in this country, including Magnolia, plane, Monkey Puzzle, larch and spruce. They died out with the ice, and only survived in warmer lands further south. When it was over, they gradually travelled back, carried by

Leaf rollers
The privet leaf in the picture was rolled by a very small caterpillar. Undo the roll and you will see the silk bands that hold it and perhaps some nicks, cut in the midrib, to help it bend. Try to watch the creature at work and see its life history. The other photograph shows a leaf rolled by a small black weevil that lays an egg in its roll of birch leaf. Undo the roll to see how the leaf was cut. Aphids (page 36) curl leaves without using silk or cuts.

Leaf eaters
These are mainly caterpillars and beetles. Look around the plant for them, especially on younger leaves nearby, but by autumn they may have gone. Small holes in beech leaves are usually made by a black jumping weevil. Young insects often scrape the leaf without making a proper hole, but neatly rounded cut-outs, especially on rose leaves, are probably made by leaf-cutter bees.

birds, by the wind, and so on. But soon Britain was cut off from Europe by water, and fewer seeds could get across. Larch and Norway spruce did not get back till travellers brought them in the sixteenth (spruce) and the seventeenth (larch) centuries. It is hard to say if these and many others are native or introduced trees. Many of the well known trees of our parks were brought here by explorers and travellers, such as Tradescant, who brought the Tulip tree, Locust tree and Virginia creeper. Many of these foreign plants only survive if they are given special treatment, but a few of them do so well that they spread out of gardens and become naturalised. If you decide to study one of these plants, try to find where it came from, and how. Capital letters to names may mean a man's name or a place name.

Rolled

Mined

Frost and wind

Eaten

Poor light

34

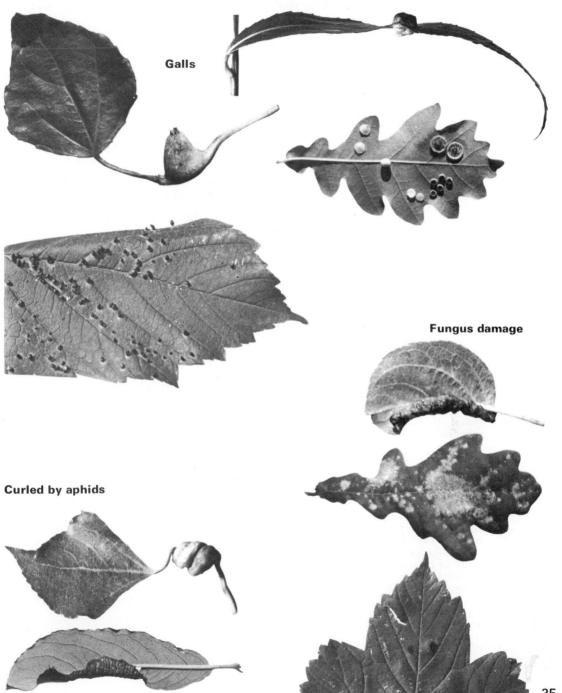

Galls

Fungus damage

Curled by aphids

35

Galls

These are swellings caused by the irritation of a little animal, usually a grub. If you open the case, you may see the grub inside, feeding on it. The

egg from which the grub hatched was laid in a slit in the plant, and the gall swelled up around it. In time, the grub will pupate and turn into a little winged insect. The three galls on this oak leaf are quite common. You can find their names and some other pictures in 'Introduction to Zoology through Nature Study' by R. Lulham. The adult insects are tiny dark wasps, but some of them do not come out of the gall till the winter is over, and as they lie on the ground through the winter, many birds like to eat them. Do the different kinds grow all over oak leaves, or does each have its special place? Oaks have other galls on the stems (page 75) and even the roots. Some, like the Oak Apple gall, are very big and have extra eggs laid in them by other wasps. Young Oak Marble galls will make black ink (once the only method) if they are rubbed with iron. Many other plants, especially wild roses, have galls. The gall on the narrow willow leaf is caused by the grub of a saw-fly, a relative of the wasps. The Pouch gall on the poplar leaf contains aphids. The Nail galls in the other picture, which are common on sycamore, are caused by very small mites.

Aphids

These little creatures may be green, black or greyish. They suck plant juices through a tube under the head, and often make young leaves curl round them. The leaf stalk of the black poplar can form a pouch or a special curl. When aphids suck plant juices, they get more sugary food than they need, and give it out in sticky drops that fall from the hind end. This 'honey dew' often falls on to other leaves or to the ground, and makes them sticky or grows black moulds.

Fungus Damage

There are many kinds of damage due to fungus but these three are very common: the whitish Oak Mildew, the red Peach Leaf Curl (also on other trees) and the black Tarspot of sycamore. Early in the year, the Tarspot patches are white. Fungus damage weakens the tree, and is infectious. Toadstools are another kind of fungus, and some toadstools feed on tree trunks.

Protection of plants from pests by ants and sugar glands

Ants like sugar and they are also very fierce little animals that will kill many of the insects you find on plants, such as caterpillars, and eat them. This is very easy to see, and so is their love for sugar. Drop a few grains near a nest and they will soon cluster round. Ants take honey dew from the hind ends of aphids, as you can see if you watch them on a plant. They protect them and kill the many predators that eat aphids. By July, aphids are usually controlled by predators unless they are protected by ants. So the ants are a nuisance to gardeners in this respect.

But a number of plants, like almond, cherry, Guelder rose and Cherry laurel have little bumps on the leaves and stalks that seem to be sugar glands. You can often see that ants are interested in them (and sometimes the bees are, also). Perhaps the plants find it useful to attract ants, since they are so fierce with caterpillars and other pests. Test this out, if you can, and see if the trees with sugar glands have less damage from pests than other trees.

Horsechestnut

Check. The leaves grow in pairs and can be very large. They usually have 5–7 leaflets, whose sizes vary. The twigs are thick and the buds become sticky, in time. The flowers are in big upright sprays, and the fruits are greenish cases with big brown seeds (conkers) inside.

*** The lowest branches, if they have not been lopped, grow down and then up in an S-shaped curve, as do those of many other trees. The leaf scars are large and clear, with the marks of the veins placed like the nails of a horse shoe. As the buds open the young leaves are protected by fluff and by folding. The flowers are large and interesting, and sometimes the honey-guides change colour. They mainly attract bumble bees. Only the lowest flowers of a spike have proper pistils which turn into fruits: the stages are easy to find. The flowers on the upper part of the spike have tiny useless pistils, and their part of the stem is often cast off neatly about July. Conkers (pages 29 and 30) can be soaked in hot water to soften them. Then you can take them apart to see the parts of the seed. To get a really hard conker that will break the others, you need to do the reverse, and dry it out slowly. The patterns of the autumn leaves are colourful and varied, and the leaflets fall separately. They decay fast, so it is easy to watch the stages.

Virginia creeper

Check. This climber has side branchlets that either coil or grow little climbing pads like those on page 76.

*** The autumn colours are brilliant. Try to compare sunlit and shaded leaves.

Wild broom

Check. The leaves are very small and fall early, leaving the bush with the green stems as shown on page 46. The upper leaves are like Spanish broom. The flowers are like yellow pea-flowers. Spanish broom has only simple leaves, without leaflets, and flowers of several colours. Gorse has spines.

*** Try to see how new flowers explode their pollen when a bee lands on them. Try to explode one yourself. Look for the pistils inside, and see how they grow into pods.
You may hear them explode when they get very dry (page 27). Compare wild plants with the cultivated ones in parks, and try to grow the seeds.

Laburnum

Check. Most of the leaves are clustered on dwarf shoots. The flowers are like small yellow pea-flowers and hang down in a chain. The laburnum tree has rather smooth olive-brown bark, often with diamond shaped rough patches.

*** There are clear wrinkles where a branch joins the stem, and they droop to form 'chinese beards'. You can often see the series from flower to fruit on one spray, but many flowers fall without producing fruits. Old fruit pods (page 27) often stay on the tree a long time. The black seeds are poisonous. In spring, look for the seedlings germinating, and see whether they travel far from the tree. Young leaves have small wings at the base, and sometimes you can find leaves with extra leaflets. The bud scales are very small, with silver hairs, and often have a tiny triple leaf on top. The dwarf shoots have close-packed girdle scars, so you can find their age. They often fork, with the remains of a flower in the angle. If you look closely at the bark you may see how it peels off in small thin layers of brownish cork, leaving a greener colour underneath. The heart wood is unusual.

Cut-leaved maple

Check. The leaves grow in pairs on thin twigs. This small tree is often called Japanese Maple, and there are other kinds with deep lobes instead of leaflets.

*** The spring and autumn colours are very beautiful. Compare this with other maples and sycamores.

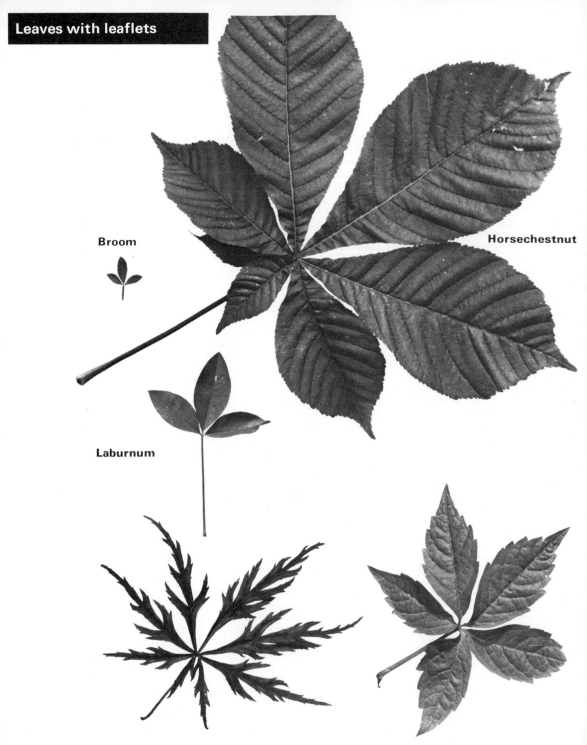

Broom

Horsechestnut

Laburnum

38 Cut-leaved maple

Virginia creeper

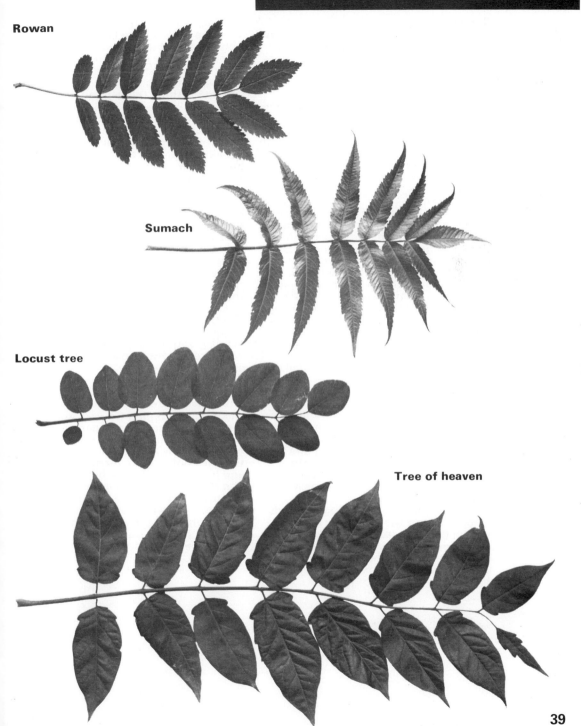

Rowan

Sumach

Locust tree

Tree of heaven

39

Rowan

Check. These large leaves do not grow in pairs, and their leaflets have very clear teeth. The small whitish flowers grow in clusters and are followed by bunches of green, then red, berries. A similar tree with fewer, very big berries, is the cultivated Service Tree.

*** The leaves have brilliant autumn colours and the lenticels of the twigs stretch as they grow. Some people call this tree the Mountain ash. Compare it with the true ash and see if you think this a good name.

Sumach

Check. These very big leaves are paler underneath. They grow on a bush with thick furry stems and upright furry-looking flower heads.

*** The flower heads grow into reddish brown fruit clusters, but in this country we have few or no pollen trees, so the fruits do not usually contain proper seed. New bushes are easily grown from suckers, and the autumn colours are very fine.

Locust tree

Check. The leaflets of young trees can be more rounded than in this picture. The stalks of the leaflets look rather thick and green from underneath, and they move the leaflet according to the weather. The leaves themselves are not in pairs. Each may have two spines at the base, which are soft and small at first. The pea-shaped flowers hang in chains, usually white, and are followed by large pods. Old trees have rather shaggy, soft bark splitting into a deep lattice of irregular furrows. Bladder Senna is a bush with similar leaves with blunt tops, but the flowers are yellow and the pods very bladder-like (page 27).

*** This tree is also called Robinia or False acacia. The buds are buried in the remains of the leaf-base during the winter, and hard to find. In spring they seem to burst out of the stem itself, and the unfolding of the leaflets is interesting. Some trees have many burrs on the trunk, and the branches may zig-zag like the oak. The seeds will often grow, and sometimes you can find suckers.

Tree of heaven

Check. This tree is also called Ailanthus. The leaves are very large and do not grow in pairs. The leaflets often number more than twenty and do not always grow in exact pairs: often there is no leaflet at the tip. Each leaflet has two or more teeth at the base, and each tooth has a green spot underneath.

*** The green spots are sugar glands (page 36), and they are very clear on young, growing leaves, which will also show you why there is sometimes no leaflet at the tip. The youngest leaflets are covered with red hairs.

The flowers are small and green, in clusters, and pollen flowers and seed flowers grow on separate trees. The fruits each have one seed in the *middle* of a wing, but in this country they are not usually fertile. The twigs and leaf scars are very big and clear. The bark is woolly on young twigs, but older bark has pale splits in summer. The seeds were first sent to this country in the early eighteenth century, by a French missionary in China, named D'Incarville.

Elder

Check. The leaves can be quite large, with five or seven leaflets. They grow in pairs and often have tiny wings at the base. The winter buds are never very neatly packed, and are often greenish and half undone by the end of the winter. The small flowers are white and scented, and arranged in a flat plate. The small berries are black, in bunches.

*** Some of the leaves turn unusual colours in autumn, and the juice of the berries will dye wool. Elderberry jelly is made by cooking the berries with apple, filtering the juice through cloth, adding a pound of sugar to a pint of juice and boiling till it is ready to set. Birds eat the berries greedily. Look for the purple splashes that their pellets make, as a result. Will any seeds grow from them? Inside thick young stems there is a wide pith that can be peeled and made into a doll that will not fall over. A rounded drawing pin is stuck into the bottom. If you need a wooden tube for model-making, you can push out the pith of an elder twig. In spring, if you look at a growing bud, you will find a series from bud scale to normal leaf. Look at the flower buds and try to make out the pattern. Does every flower form a berry?

Holly-leaved barberry

Check. This bushy plant is also called Mahonia or the Oregon grape. The leaves vary a little, but always have spiny leaflets.

*** Look for yellow flowers similar to other barberries, and for the fruits, which are rather like small grapes. Some bushes produce suckers, from which new plants can be grown.

Ash

Check. The leaves can be very large and 'leggy', and they grow in pairs. The leaflets have very small teeth, and they are joined to a deep but narrow midrib which has two ridges on top. The twigs are grey-green, rather thick, with squat black buds (page 18). The fruits grow in bunches, and each one has a twisted wing, with a seed at the stalk end. The little stalks, or even the fruits, may stay on the tree all winter. The flowers come early in the year, before the leaves, and look like reddish tufts.

*** The flower tufts often fall in a high wind, and you can see the curious little flowers, with reddish stamens but no petals. If you collect those that fall a little later, you can see how the flower gradually grows into a fruit. The leaf buds open rather late but if you look at the bud scales and the lowest leaves you will see a gradual change from one shape into the other (a leaf series). You will often find seedlings under the parent tree, but some of the fruits are carried further off. The seeds will not grow in their first year, unless they were planted in autumn, while still green from the tree. Usually they have to wait for a long time in cold moist ground. The first leaves of the seedlings, even after the seed-leaves, are not like the parent. The bark of old ash trees has a pattern of regular, deep furrows, and makes a good bark-rubbing. Look for a 'weeping' variety of ash that is sometimes grown in parks.

Wisteria

Check. These large leaves do not grow in pairs, and their leaflets have stalks that look thick and green from underneath. The plant can be grown as a climber or pruned into a bush. The flowers are shaped like pea-flowers and hang in long chains. They are usually mauve.

*** This is a beautiful plant to study. The usual kind comes from China, and giant plants have been grown, with over half a million flowers.

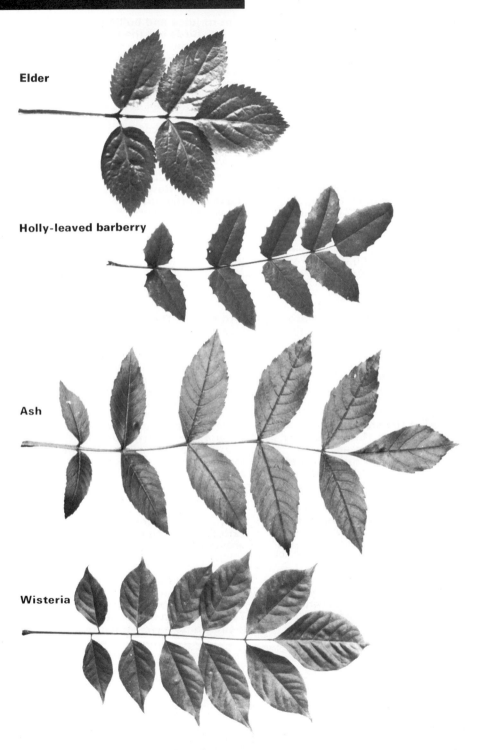

Elder

Holly-leaved barberry

Ash

Wisteria

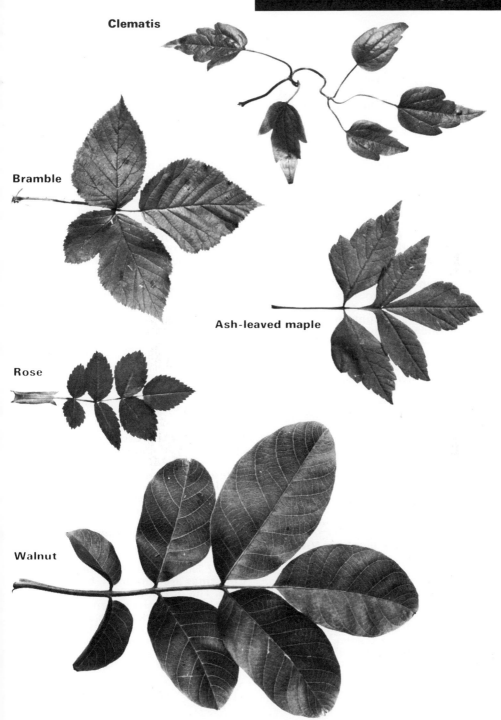

Clematis

Bramble

Ash-leaved maple

Rose

Walnut

43

Clematis

Check. The leaf stalks are used for clinging. Cultivated flowers vary, but wild ones have four petals and flower late. The fruits are in little bunches, with fluffy tails. Other names are Travellers Joy and Old Man's Beard.

*** Is the fluff on the seeds any use? Test out your ideas, and try growing the seeds. They are said to do best on chalky soil.

The bark is shaggy and birds may take it for nests. Peel and scrape a branch, and you will find that the woody centre is in several strands,

not a solid lump. It is like the wire in an electric flex. Does this make the stem able to bend more, without

breaking? Does it need to bend? Read how similar tropical lianes were used by jungle bridge builders, and for dangerous jumping ('Quest in Paradise', by D. Attenborough).

Bramble

Check. There are small hooks under the main veins and on the stems, and they help in scrambling over other plants. There are usually three or five leaflets. The fruits are blackberries, with clusters of tiny juicy fruits above a ring of sepals. Raspberry plants are similar but the berries are red, the stems are more upright and the leaves are pale underneath.

*** The white or pink flowers are fairly large, in loose clusters, and you can follow the growth of the fruits and the way they change colour. Each tiny fruit has a patterned wooden case inside, with a seed. Blackberry jelly is messy to make but has a strong flavour. Look at the long arched stems and see if any of them will root at the tip.

Ash-leaved maple

Check. The leaves vary in shape but usually have five leaflets, and grow in pairs. The fruit is like droopy sycamore. The tree really is a kind of maple, but the leaves are similar to

the ash and elder, giving the other name Box elder. A variegated variety is grown in gardens.

*** See the notes for sycamore and maples on page 72, and compare them.

Rose

Check. Rose leaves vary in size and in the number of leaflets, but they all have wings at the base, very like those in the picture, but sometimes fringed. Some rose leaves have hooks on the midribs, and wild roses hold themselves up with hooks on the stems.

*** Rosehips have plenty of Vitamin

C, which helps protect us from disease. If you open a rose hip you will find hairy fruits inside, and a round hole at the top, between the sepals. Try to find this hole in the flower. Many insects live on wild roses. You may find round galls and fluffy galls, leaves cut by leaf-cutting bees (page 36) and mines made by fly grubs in the hips.

Walnut

Check. The leaves are large with regular veins. In summer you can often see the walnuts on the tree, in large green cases.

*** Take apart a fresh walnut or one bought early in the season, to see the parts of the seed (page 29). Will they

grow? The walnuts sold near Christmas are kiln dried, brittle and dead. The opening buds are a fine sight in spring, the pollen catkins are very big. The bark at one stage has diamond-shaped patches but later becomes fissured and has pale corky layers in it.

Larch

Check. Most of the leaves grow in bunches on dwarf shoots, and are a little over an inch long. They look like needles, but do not feel stiff. The seed catkins look like small pink roses and grow into brown cones smaller than a fir-cone, with rather papery scales that do not fit closely.

The main branches of big trees slant down, with the smaller branches hanging almost vertically from them.

*** This unusual conifer is deciduous, and worth seeing in spring and autumn. Look for the pollen catkins in spring, and the bright new leaves. Squirrels often tear the cones apart and throw down the remains, but very few fall naturally, so it is difficult to find the seeds between the scales.

Cypress

Check. The leaves are very tiny scales, pressed against the twigs in slightly different patterns for different kinds. The closed cones are small and almost round, with far fewer scales than a fir cone, and each scale has a wide top.

If the cone is oval, not round, the tree is a near relation called thuja.
*** There are seeds between the scales and the usual foliage is fern like, making good plaster casts. The tree has a beautiful natural shape but is often clipped. The bark peels off older trunks.

Tamarisk

Check. This small tree or bush also has tiny leaves, but it has proper flowers, small and pinkish on long sprays.
*** Look out for this at the seaside. It is one of the few bushes that can stand salt spray. Can you find any others?

Cedar

Check. There are several kinds of cedar, e.g. the deodar and cedar of Lebanon. Most of the evergreen needles are under one inch long and arranged in stiff tufts on dwarf shoots. They are sometimes a bluish green. The cedar of Lebanon is often grown on park lawns and has strong low horizontal branches with the small branches arranged like a plate. The cones are big, hard and rounded, with a smooth outline, as the scales fit neatly. The name 'cedar' is often given to American trees that are not true cedars.
*** Look for the pollen cones, which come late, and try giving the branch a slight shake. The bark and the smell are different from other trees.

Pine

Check. The needle-like leaves are quite long and are bound together, usually in two's or three's, that fall off together. There are several different pines, all evergreens.

*** Look for pollen cones, small seed cones and for young needles, in spring. Look for stages in growth of the seed cones, for they take two years to ripen. See the effect of dampness and dryness on the ripe cones, and look for seeds. The bark on young trees and big branches is reddish, breaking off in 'scoops' at a paler softer layer. Compare this with older trees and very young branches. The branches on a young tree grow in whorls (before they start to fall off) and if you look at fresh deal planks (pinewood or a similar wood) you can see traces of these branches in some of them. Pine is said to need well-drained soil and plenty of light. Does your tree have these? Birch and pine forests were important to the men of the Middle Stone Age, as the climate was unsuitable for most other trees. You can find in books how these men lived in the forest and what they made.

Broom

Check. These twigs with five narrow ridges have already lost their leaves.
*** See page 37. Try rolling a wet stem across a small piece of Plasticine.

45

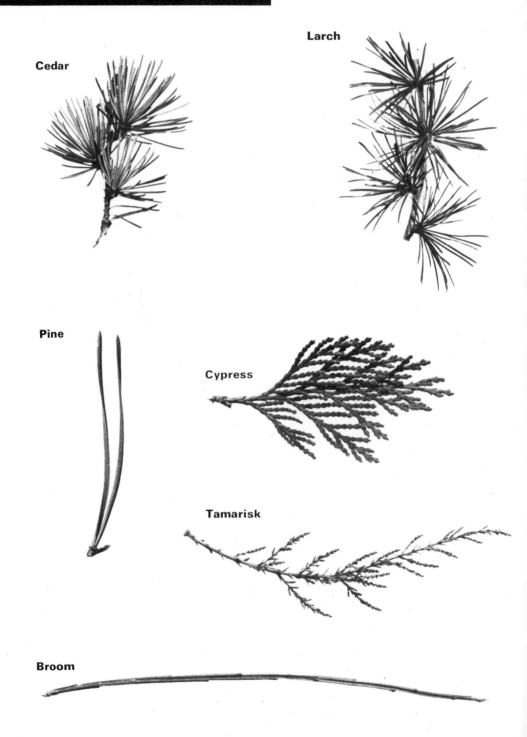

Cedar

Larch

Pine

Cypress

Tamarisk

Broom

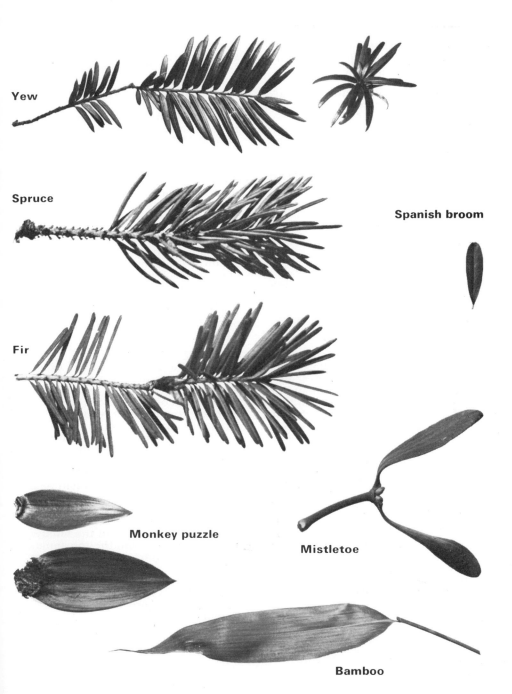

Yew

Spruce

Spanish broom

Fir

Monkey puzzle

Mistletoe

Bamboo

47

Yew

Check. The leaves have a midrib *sticking up* on top. Vertical stems have leaves all round, but horizontal stems have them in two rows, forming a very good fishbone mosaic. The ripe seeds are quite large, and each has a juicy cup which turns pink. (If your tree has cones it may be Canadian Redwood or Western Hemlock.)
*** In spring, look for pollen catkins, (usually on a separate tree), and for the stages of the seeds. See which birds take the seeds, but be careful, for the seeds are poisonous, and the leaves are poisonous to animals. Try to see an old yew trunk. The wood is the most elastic we have: try to test it for rebound and find out how bows are made.

Spanish broom

See page 37 for broom.

Mistletoe

Check. This is not really a tree, but a small plant *growing on* a tree, often apple or hawthorn, and getting most of its food that way. The leaves are thick, and grow in pairs. The whole plant branches many times and forms a rounded clump.
*** The flowers are very small and greenish. On some plants there are pollen flowers and on others, seed flowers, so half our mistletoe has no berries. If you find mistletoe on a tree, look further along the branch for tiny sprouts. It travels along inside the branch sending up shoots at intervals. Watch how much the plant grows in a year. Try planting berries on apple tree bark, but not if you value the tree very much. Do not expect quick results.

Bamboo

Check. The 'blades' of these leaves can grow quite large, but there is also a lower part of each leaf that wraps closely round the stem. When this tubular part of the leaf is pulled off it makes a circular scar all round the stem.
*** This is not a real shrub, for all

Spruce

Check. The needles never form a real fishbone mosaic like the Yew, for some of them cover the stem. When the needles fall naturally, each leaves a tiny stalk or peg on the twig. There are several kinds of spruce and they are often used for Christmas trees. The cones are made of hard leaflike pieces, and are often very long.
*** Look for the different stages and parts, as for pine (page 45). This wood is often used for plywood: try to see some. The trees were brought here in 1548 but they were not used as Christmas trees till much later.

Fir

Check. There are several kinds of fir tree and they may have two rows of needles on each side of the stem, or the stem may be hidden by needles. When the needles fall they do not leave a peg, so the stem is fairly smooth. The cones are long or short, but they usually have little pointed pieces poking out between the scales.
*** Look for the various stages and parts as for pine, page 45.

Monkey Puzzle

Check. This is also called the Chile pine or araucaria. The hard pointed leaves stay on the tree for many years, and cover most of the branches all over, so a monkey would not climb very easily.
*** Look for the regular whorls of the upper branches, and the beautiful spirals made by the leaves. Old trees, with cones, are uncommon. In summer, you may find resin where the bark splits.

new stems come from the base. It is really a giant grass, and the hollow stems never thicken, though some are big from the start. Look at bamboo canes and at a big grass, to compare. Look at the leaves of bamboo on a dry day and try to see Chinese or Japanese paintings of it. It rarely flowers.

Elm

Check. This is an elm fruit, not a leaf (page 60), but the fruits grow quite large before the leaves unfold.

*** The fruits of the common elm are not fertile. Look for the wing of the fruit, the position of the seed, and the remains of stigmas, stamens and sepals.

Ivy

Check. Ivy leaves shaped like this are *usually* only found on plants growing high up, and about to flower, but some cultivated and variegated kinds *always* have this shape. (See page 73.)

Lilac

Check. The Latin name for lilac is Syringa, but most people use the name 'Syringa' for the shrub on page 57. The two plants have been confused ever since they were brought here, together, from Turkey, in 1562. Lilac leaves grow in pairs, and they are usually curved, not flat. The green winter buds are also in pairs, even at the tip of the stem, where you will find a dead bud in between.

The flowers are usually white or mauve ('lilac'), and have four petals except for double varieties. Each flower is small, but they are usually arranged in big, double clusters.

*** Old bushes have shaggy bark, and you may find that the birds will take it for nest building.

The twigs fork a lot, just like the flower clusters, and you can see the reason if you watch the growing buds. The opening buds have a series from bud scales to the ordinary leaf, and the young leaves are rolled together. The twigs stop growing and form winter buds very early, often in May. In summer, when the weather is dry, the leaves at the top of the bush roll up perhaps to keep moist. The fruits are flat cases with seeds inside (page 27). See how they open, and try to grow the seeds. Cuttings are often successful.

Lime

Check. This picture shows the wing of the fruit, which is yellowish or brown, and usually has flowers or fruits attached. The ordinary leaf is on page 58.

*** The flowers have petals and sepals, and plenty of nectar and scent that attract many bees. The fruits sail down on their wings about August (page 21). The number of fruits to a wing can vary. Which is the commonest number, and is it the same for every tree? Aphids often drip honey dew on the leaves and the ground. Shaded leaves turn bright yellow and fall in summer. The wood has an even grain and the bast is strong and elastic, especially when damp. It can be used for mats or for rope to tie the poles of a hut together. The bark turns silvery, often with pinkish lenticels, and then splits into a lacy silvery network, but this does not show when it is wet. Old trees have deep splits, often along a line of lenticels. This tree is not the same as the tropical lime, which has fruits like green lemons.

The bud scales (page 18) open early and turn pink where the sunlight falls. Each leaf has two scales. The young shoots droop at first, but rise up later, and the leaves make a very good fishbone mosaic. Is the bigger leaf lobe always on the same side? When the twigs stop growing in summer, the tips drop off. Severely pruned trees grow burrs and unusual leaves with big teeth or funnels. Branches often root if the tip is held against the earth (layering).

Catalpa

Check. The leaves are very large and have a felty layer underneath, that you can feel. The twigs are thick, with deep-oval leaf-scars. The flowers are large and white, with yellow and pink honey-guides. The fruits are long thin twig-like pods.

*** Every part is so large that this tree is well worth study, but it starts very late in spring. It is often called Indian Bean, but comes from other countries, too.

Barberry

See page 65.

Lime

Elm

Ivy

Catalpa

Barberry

Lilac

50

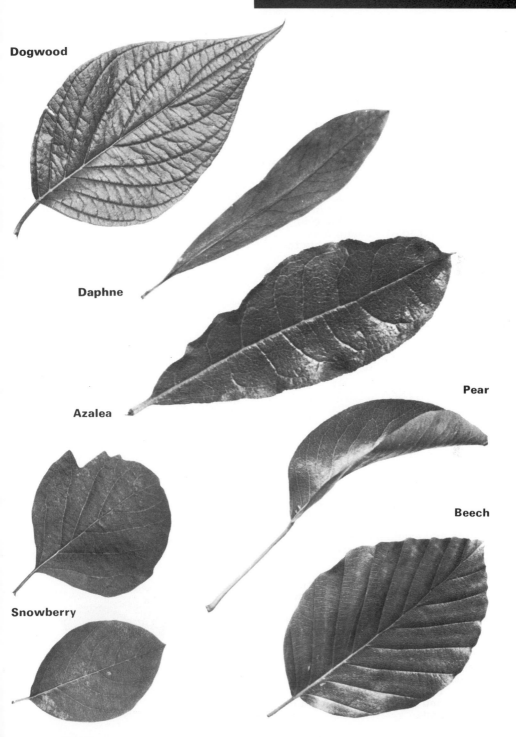

Dogwood

Daphne

Azalea

Pear

Snowberry

Beech

51

Pear
See page 65.

Beech
Check. The leaves have a silky fringe when they are young. The winter buds are long, thin, pointed and stick out from the stem (page 18). The bark is rather smooth and silvery, even on big trees. The fruits are small, brown, edible nuts, each with three sharp edges. They grow in pairs, in four-rayed prickly cases (page 28). In most years there are very few good nuts.
*** Branch wrinkles and seals are very plain on young trees. Many beech trees were coppiced in the past, and have grown into a clump of trunks instead of a single one. Very few green plants are able to grow under beech. See how many you can find. The autumn colours are beautiful. The leaves and bud scales decay only slowly, so there is usually a thick brown layer under beech trees. The tree sends short fat fungus roots into this leaf mould for mineral

fertiliser. Each fungus-root is made partly of tree root and partly of fungus. In autumn, the fungus part grows out into toadstools, which are common under beech. Sometimes you can also find a tiny white cup-fungus growing on damp old prickly cases. The opening buds are beautiful in spring and each leaf has two long thin bud scales. There are pollen catkins and small seed catkins on the same tree. The lowest branches have such a good leaf mosaic that they cut off the light and keep off the rain. You will get a surprise if you try to find the age of some of these small low twigs by girdle scars. Young leaves often have mines (page 34) with a grub or cocoon inside. If you keep them a small black jumping weevil will come out and eat the leaves. Beech seedlings have large fan-shaped seed leaves and can grow in the shade.

Dogwood
Check. The leaves vary in width but always have very curved veins and no teeth. Variegated dogwoods are grown in parks. The small white flowers have four petals and grow in clusters. One kind has four white leaves round each bunch of flowers. The berries are usually black.
*** The winter twigs and buds are unusual. You may find suckers, but the seeds are slow to grow.

Daphne
Check. There are several Daphnes, but this one is a small bush with most of the leaves in tufts, at the ends of the twigs.
*** The red berries are very poisonous. The mauve flowers come early, before the leaves.

Azalea
Check. This is really a kind of rhododendron. The leaves of big azaleas are usually deciduous, with a fringe of stiff hairs. The flowers are big and showy, like other rhododendrons (page 53).
*** The flower and stamens are worth study. See how many different colours you can find in parks and gardens. The fruit is a hard case with seeds inside, and it opens as it dries. Azalea plants will only grow well if the soil is acid. In spring the big buds are worth watching as they open their dark-tipped scales. Flowering, evergreen azaleas, are often sold at Christmas, and Japanese evergreen azaleas are small plants.

Snowberry
Check. These leaves grow in pairs on the thin upper twigs of the bush, with the tiny pink flowers at the tips.

Another kind of leaf, with lobes (page 74), will be found on long shoots.

Privet

Check. The biggest leaves of the wild privet are quite narrow, but the biggest leaves of the cultivated Japanese privets are much wider. The leaves grow in pairs and some of the cultivated kinds are variegated or yellow.

*** The leaf veins form loops, seen against the light. In April you can find a leaf series on each twig, going from bud scale, through short rounded leaves to fully shaped ones. The stem often stops growing in late spring and forms a brown scaly 'winter' bud. If the hedge is clipped, this 'winter' bud will often grow out, so there may be two leaf series on one stem, and an extra girdle scar. Look for leaf rollers and leaf miners and see what they do. Sometimes you can find a twig with leaves in threes. Look on unpruned bushes and parts of bushes for the white, strongly-scented flowers, and try to work out the pattern in which they are arranged, and the numbers of petals and stamens. Are there more flowers in sun or in shade? The flowers are followed by small black poisonous berries. If a hedge is being cut down, try to see inside it and look at the pattern the clipped twigs make. Sometimes you can see the shape of an earlier hedge inside. When twigs grow upright, the leaves are in pairs at right angles, but look for horizontal twigs with a fishbone mosaic, and twigs in darker places with the leaves in a rosette. Sometimes you can find strong new branches from low down, with the leaves wide apart, and growing very fast and very long. Old stems often have white lenticels and thin layers of shaggy cork. Try growing cuttings. Which grows faster, golden or green privet?

Holly

See page 73.

Rhododendron

Check. These thick, evergreen leaves grow on a bush. They vary a little in shape, and some have a brown felt underneath. The flowers grow in clusters, and have large petals joined to make a trumpet shape.

*** Look under the bush for skeleton leaves, and try to find out when the leaves fall. The flowers are large and you can see all the parts clearly. Look for honey guides and for the unusual way the stamens open. See how many different colours you can find. The fruits are hard cases, with seeds inside. Some of our best kinds of rhododendron were bred from seed, using plants brought from abroad by Robert Fortune, a famous plant collector.

Magnolia

Check. There are many Magnolias, evergreen and deciduous, bushes and trees, but the deciduous one in the picture is very popular. The beautiful flowers are always large and pale, with separate petals. In the centre, they always have a cluster of thin pistils, not just one.

*** The flower buds are large, often with hairy bud-scales. Look for the fruits, and try to find skeleton leaves on the ground under evergreen magnolias. They are also sold by florists as 'shadow leaves'. Magnolias are very ancient plants that lived even in the time of the dinosaurs. Try to see pictures of these. Books will tell you about the wild Magnolias that once grew in Britain, and also where our garden Magnolias came from.

Cultivated privet

Wild privet

Holly

Rhododendron

Magnolia

54

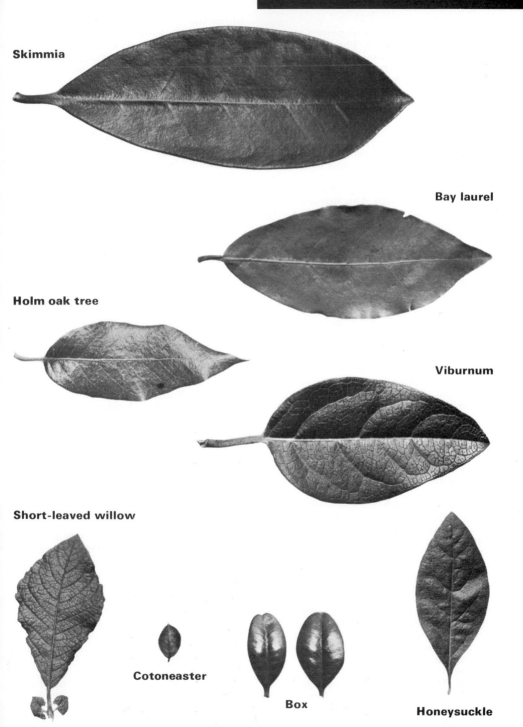

Skimmia

Bay laurel

Holm oak tree

Viburnum

Short-leaved willow

Cotoneaster

Box

Honeysuckle

55

Bay laurel

Check. The leaves are unpaired and have a pleasant smell. They grow on a large tree or a pruned bush.

✳✳✳ Compare with the bay-leaves sold for cooking. This is probably the *real* laurel, used in ancient Greece. Another name is Sweet bay. The spring flowers are small and whitish. Some trees produce black berries, others only pollen.

Viburnum

There are many different kinds of viburnum, and this one was often called Laurustinus.

Check. The paired evergreen leaves grow on dark stalks. The flowers are very small, white, clustered, each with five petals, and they often come out in winter.

✳✳✳ The plant is often grown from cuttings. Look at the other kinds of viburnum in this book.

Box

Check. The small paired leaves are evergreen. Box grows as a bush, a tree or a close-clipped edging plant, as in Elizabethan gardens. The small pale flowers hide among the leaves.

✳✳✳ The wood is very fine-grained, and so heavy that it sinks in water. Try to see a boxwood top or ruler. The wood is also used for wood engraving (end grain) and fine carving.

Honeysuckle

Check. The paired leaves are usually rather woolly when young, and the stem will twine round a support. The flowers are usually pink and yellow, in small bunches. They have long tubes and a strong scent, but no platform for insects to land on. The fruits are red, partly transparent berries, in clusters and seem to be poisonous. Garden (foreign) honeysuckles may be different in many ways.

✳✳✳ See if the stems always twine the same way: they can 'choke' the support. The leaves may have more than one side bud each. The flowers are supposed to be visited in the evening by hovering moths, with long tongues and a good sense of smell. Are most of the flowers pollinated? Look at a cluster of berries and see how many have grown. The bark has loose shaggy mesh-work strips, and you often see the birds tugging at it. Look for bark in old birds nests. Honeysuckle does not seem to flower well in shady places.

Skimmia

Check. The leaves of this skimmia have red stalks but there are others. They are paler underneath, with tiny dark dots, and the side-veins are hard to see. The edge of the leaf is bevelled. The flowers have four narrow, white petals, and some produce red berries similar to aucuba, some only pollen.

✳✳✳ The stages from flower to fruit are easy to see. Hold the leaf up to the light and you see a thin transparent edge and very tiny light dots all over. New plants are grown from cuttings.

Holm oak tree

Check. These tough evergreen leaves are rather felty below, and they vary in size and shape, often with teeth (page 66), often wavy or curling under. The leaf stalk and small twigs are hairy. The fruits are acorns.

✳✳✳ Look for the long pollen catkins in spring. The young pistils are small knobs on little stalks, growing near the ends of the branches. Cork oak is similar to Holm oak except for the bark.

Short-leaved willow

Check. The different kinds of willow are hard to distinguish, but the sallow or Pussy willow is a common short-leaved one of wet and acid places. The flowers are on short catkins with silky hairs: pollen catkins on one bush, seed catkins on another. The winter buds have only one scale going right round them. The leaves are not paired and they have wings at the base.

✳✳✳ Bees visit the early willows but some pollen is carried by the wind, too. The fruits of many willows ripen early and give out fluffy seeds (page 23) which must be planted at once, to grow. Trees are often grown from cuttings. Try a twig in water.

Cotoneaster

Check. There are several different kinds of cotoneaster. They have no thorns though the red berries resemble the fire-thorn. Some varieties grow low, with a fish-bone arrangement of leaves. The flowers are small and pale.

✳✳✳ Look for different kinds and patterns, and compare the names in a gardening book. Try to grow cuttings and seeds.

Syringa
Check. The leaves grow in pairs and vary in width. The flowers have four large white petals and a strong scent. They are often called 'Mock orange', but the correct Latin name is Philadelphus.
*** Is it *really* like lilac? (page 49). Look for the fruits and the side-buds.

Birch
Check. The leaves can grow big on shaded trees and are slightly different on young trees. The twigs are delicate and often hang down. The bark is white in the middle stage of the tree's life, giving the name White birch.
*** Is the name 'Silver' birch accurate? The white bark has thin corky layers, peeling across. They contain wax and can be used to start a camp fire, but only if they are thin and peel easily without cutting the tree. The lenticels are big and the branch wrinkles are clear and black on young trees. Look at the bark of *very* young and very old trees, and try to see or make a birch broom. Look near birch trees in autumn for a red and white poisonous toadstool. It is connected by fine threads to the birch roots (fungus roots, page 52). Another big white fungus often grows out from the trunk, like a shelf. It is a parasite. Bunches of twigs, called witches brooms, are caused by fungus or mites. The birch also has leaf miners, leaf rollers (page 33) and other insects. Look in parks and books for the American paper birch and the one used for Red Indians' canoes. The long pollen catkins grow before the leaves, but the small green seed catkins stand upright among the young leaves. Look for the little red stigmas, and see the catkin turn down as the fruits ripen. What happens to the pollen catkins? In autumn, break up a ripe catkin and see the fruits (page 22). They travel long distances. You can find them on anything sticky, in spiders' webs, or among dead leaves. They need to be planted as soon as they are ripe. Grow some of the seeds to recognise the tiny seedlings on page 30. Then look for seedlings and young trees everywhere on open ground, coke piles and moss patches. They nearly always get in before other trees.

Black poplar
Check. These tough leaves are flat, and have the leaf stalk flattened *sideways.* The buds are rather long and sometimes sticky. They grow on pale knobbly twigs. One variety, the Lombardy poplar, has the branches growing straight up. The fruits ripen early and give out a cloud of fluffy seeds, which need planting at once. Some trees produce fluff but no real seeds.

Some fallen leaves have a swollen or twisted stalk with aphids inside (page 35). Old trees have deeply fissured bark. In summer, some of the twigs are neatly cut off at the swollen base. Try rolling twigs across Plasticine. When the buds open, the leaves are rolled up, at first, and reddish. The big catkins come out early and are often found on the ground. Pollen catkins, with red stamens, are on separate trees from seed catkins.

Mulberry
Check. The leaf is similar to the lime, but thicker, downy underneath, rough on top, and less lop-sided. The fruit looks much like a loganberry or a long purple blackberry. This is the black mulberry. The white mulberry, which is less common but better for silkworms, is very similar but has whitish fruits and smooth leaves.
*** The flowers and fruit are really rather different from loganberry and blackberry. Silkworm eggs can be bought from dealers.

Lime
Check. There are several slightly different kinds of lime, with different leaf sizes. The leaf is bigger on one side than the other. The flowers come late, hanging in small bunches from a yellow-green special leaf (seen on page 50). For more details see page 49.

Black poplar

Syringa

Birch

Mulberry

Lime

Wych elm

Elm

Hornbeam

Hazel

Alder

Elms

Check. The leaves usually feel rough and are lop-sided at the base. Wych elm leaves are larger, with a narrower point and sometimes two extra-large teeth. Common elm leaves are wavy, unless they grow in the shade. Though the twigs are delicate, the main branches are rather thick and few. The lower branches are often lopped off, as in this drawing, and many people think this is the 'normal' elm shape. The trunk and main branches usually grow a fuzz of small twigs. There are 'weeping' varieties of Wych elm. Some of the high-up winter buds are swollen, giving a beaded look to the twigs. These buds produce a fuzz of reddish flowers in February, growing into bunches of leaf-like fruits (page 50) by April. The real leaves come later.

*** It is easy to collect a series of fallen flowers that will show how the fruit gradually grows, but common elm seeds never seem to sprout, and Wych elm must be planted quickly. Common elm grows suckers from the roots, and they can form a clump of trees or a hedge. See how far away they can grow, and look out for an unpruned tree to see the shape. The bark of the trunk shows the layers of cork and bast clearly, especially when cut across. Young branches may grow wings of cork. The inner bast is strong and flexible, especially when damp. It can be stripped from small branches and used like string.

Hornbeam tree

Check. The leaves vary in width, but are usually flat and symmetrical. They have narrow teeth, with a larger one opposite each vein. The bark is usually smooth, with a large-meshed silvery lattice over it. Older trees have fluted trunks. The fruits are nuts with triple wings (page 75) and are arranged in big catkins.

*** Look for pollarded trees and read about them. The wood is even and very hard, giving the name 'hornbeam'. Read about its former uses. The young leaves are pleated and held out like birds wings. The pollen catkins show early, but the seed catkins come later, and are smaller and nearer the tips of the twigs. Shake the pollen catkins to see the cloud of pollen. Try to collect the growth series from catkin to fruit, and look for nuts split open by hawfinches. Seedlings can usually be found under the trees in April. See if some have travelled further off.

Hazel

Check. These hairy leaves usually have a narrow tip and some slightly larger teeth. The young branches are hairy and the fruit is a hazel nut or a filbert, (a variety of hazel).

*** The long pollen catkins wait on the twigs all winter and open very early. They are often called lambs tails, and they are described in many books. The seed flowers are inside fat buds, but the red stigmas poke out. The leaves only come later. Hazel was once coppiced regularly, when there was a market for the poles that grew from the stumps.

Alder tree

Check. The leaves are tough and smooth on top, but not evergreen. They have a flattish end, and pale, prominent veins underneath. Bunches of tiny black cones often remain on the tree from previous years. The buds are blunt, often with a purplish bloom.

*** The long pollen catkins and the small seed catkins, on the same tree, are worth seeing. The pollen catkins hang, tightly pressed together, all winter, and open early, giving off clouds of pollen. Alders are said to grow best in damp places. Is this true in your neighbourhood?

Long-leaved willow
Check. There are several kinds of willow with long leaves, including the Cricket Bat willow, the osier, and the Weeping willow, with hanging branches. The leaves are quite tough, with very small teeth. The flowers are on catkins and the fruits are small greenish cases that mostly ripen early and let out fluffy seeds (page 23). Some trees only have pollen catkins. The winter buds each have only one scale all round the outside (page 18).
*** The stems are usually flexible and are used for weaving baskets. The wood is light, but strong, and the twigs often make strong charcoal. Twigs can be forced early in the year, for decoration, and will often root in water. Look at different Long-leaved willows and see the different colours of leaves and stems. The leaves have a special gall (page 36), caused by a grub that will change into a sawfly. The catkins have nectar and are visited by several kinds of early bees. Willow trees are often pollarded to grow poles, and these give the tree a tufted shape. The Short-leaved willows, on page 56, are similar in many ways.

Buddleia
Check. The leaves are in pairs and do not look tough, but they often stay on the bush all winter. The tiny flowers form carrot-shaped masses in summer, and are usually mauve, with orange centres. One less common kind has orange balls of flowers.
*** The flowers attract butterflies and you can see them unroll their tongues. The seeds are in small cases (page 27) and have a very good way of travelling, so that Buddleia can be found on waste places, bombed sites, even on walls. Look for plants in strange places, and try to grow some of the seeds.

Cherry
Check. There are several different kinds with slightly different, rather large leaves, and sugar glands on the stalk (page 36). Young leaves have two wings at the base. These are very frilly on some Japanese cherries, but soon fall off. The flowers are single or double, pink or white. Most trees have bunches of large flowers, but some have upright chains of small ones. Under each flower is a bulge, but it is an almost empty cup, with the future cherry at the base. The ripe cherry is red or black, large or small, but double flowers and lone trees usually bear no fruit.
*** Cherry has many dwarf shoots with close girdle scars and clustered leaves. There is a cluster of buds at the stem tip, and next year's flower buds can often be picked out as they are fatter. Notice how a row of Japanese cherries in a park usually opens and blooms all at the same time, but wild trees, like oak, birch and lime, do not all flower exactly at once. Try to find out about grafting, which makes these trees so much alike. The bark comes off in thin horizontal strips of cork for a long time, with the lenticels stretching. In the end, the bark changes. Resin often oozes out in late summer, when the trunk splits.

Sweet chestnut
Check. No other tree has a large leaf like this.
*** The bark is often furrowed in a spiral pattern. The catkins are very long and late, with some seed flowers at the base. The fruits are edible chestnuts. Each has a stigma at the end, which conkers do not have. Around the fruits is an extra, spiky case (page 28). The leaves often turn bright yellow in autumn.

Long-leaved willow

Buddleia

Cherry

Sweet chestnut

Evergreen spindle

Aucuba

Cherry 'laurel'

Portugal 'laurel'

Evergreen spindle

Check. The leaves grow in pairs and there are slightly different shapes and varieties, some variegated. This common hedge plant is often called privet, but the tough, toothed leaves are quite different. It comes from Japan and is a kind of Euonymus.

Aucuba

Check. Many different trees are called 'laurel', but it is best to keep the name for the laurel that made the victors' crowns in ancient Greece. Aucuba is different. The leaves are thick, evergreen and sometimes spotted with yellow. They grow in pairs and some of them have very few teeth. If you keep a picked leaf it often turns quite black. The stems stay green a long time, and the bush can grow in shady places. The red berries ripen late and last until the spring, but are not found on all bushes. The others are usually pollen bushes.
*** The branches fork a great deal.

Cherry 'laurel'

Check. The leaves are not in pairs and the teeth may be very small, even missing. The edge of the leaf often rolls under, and the tip nearly always turns down. Under the leaf there are two or more small patches that give out a sugary liquid in spring (see nectar glands, page 36). When the bush is not pruned, it has many upright chains of white flowers, followed by small black cherries. It is really an evergreen cherry.

Portugal 'laurel'

Check. The leaves are flat and not paired. They are smaller and darker than Cherry 'laurel', with slim, reddish stalks. The flowers and fruit resemble Cherry 'laurel' but come later (flowers in June). The two plants are closely related to each other and to ordinary cherries.
*** Compare carefully with aucuba, Cherry 'laurel' and other cherries.

*** Occasional twigs grow in threes. The flowers only grow on unpruned bushes, and have pale green stiff petals. The twigs have a leaf series, with slightly narrower ones at the tip. New plants are grown from cuttings, and the bush is often attacked by tent-building caterpillars.

See what you can find in the angles. Look at the seed inside the berry, to see the parts, and try growing some. Do birds take the berries? (This is a Japanese tree.) In spring you can see a series from the bud scales to the young leaves. When do the old leaves fall? The April flowers are green and chocolate coloured, and the parts are fairly easy to make out. Look for the pollen flowers and seed flowers on different bushes. There seem to be no pollen bushes with mottled leaves. Try to see the stages from bud to berry. Which open first, pollen or seed flowers? Are there any other differences?

*** Look for branches with a fishbone mosaic, and in spring, look for unpruned bushes with flowers. The crushed leaf has a smell and contains a poison. The vapour from young chopped leaves can be used to kill insects (see Patterns of Life, by A. Dale). Does the poison seem to protect the plant from leaf-eating insects? The leaves are used for 'laurel' wreaths in this country, but are not the true laurel.

Plum

Check. The leaves vary on the different kinds of wild and cultivated plums, including bullace, damsons, greengages, and copper-leaved plums, which have pink flowers. The others have white. Blackthorn is much the same as wild plum, but smaller. The fruits of all plums have short stalks and one big stone inside, but colours and sizes vary (page 26). .

✱✱✱ Open the stone of the fruit, to see the parts of the seed. Look for gum at injured places. Suckers often grow out of the roots. Look round the tree, even on lawns and paths, and see how far away they can grow.

Pear

Check. The leaves are similar to plum and apple, but have longer stalks and often curve as in this picture. Sometimes the teeth are very small and few. In autumn, the leaves may turn almost black. The white flowers open early in spring and have red stamens. Wild pear trees may have round fruits, and spines at the ends of twigs. Old trees often have tall branches growing straight up in the air, from the middle of the tree, and they bend over later.

✱✱✱ Look at the flower, fruit, and seeds and compare the details with the apple (next column). Pears do not make good jelly, and the flesh is gritty. The bark of old trees often breaks into neat squares, and the young leaves are double-rolled in the bud.

Holm oak tree
See page 56.

Firethorn

Check. This bush is often called pyracantha. There are several kinds, all with evergreen leaves, and some twigs ending in thorns. The berries are red or orange.

✱✱✱ Look for different kinds. See if birds eat the berries, and try growing the seeds. Look for the small pale flowers in spring.

Apple tree

Check. The leaves are similar to plum and pear but usually less pointed. The fruit always has a dent at the stalk, but there are different kinds, some very small. The twigs and buds are slightly hairy. The flowers are quite large with five petals, often pinkish, and yellow stamens.

✱✱✱ Most flowers and fruits grow on short shoots that are many years old, judging by girdle scars. Look for apples with colour patches caused by leaf shading. Cut a fruit as on page 24. Open seeds (pips) to see the parts, and try to grow some. Find out how to make apple jelly. Try drying apples. Slice them thinly, removing bad parts, dip them in salt water, then dry them in a warm place till they are like chamois leather. Store them dry and soak before cooking. Apple leaves are often attacked by mildew and Peach Leaf Curl (fungus, page 35). The bark of old trees often forms neat squares. Look at the winter buds and try to tell which will have flowers. Look at the flowers to see the solid lump underneath, where the fruit will come, and follow its growth. Try to find different kinds of apple, both as trees and in the shops. The tiny wild apples are called crabs, but there are also trees from stray pips, and some small ones grown for decoration, as well as cookers and eaters.

Beech
See page 52.

Barberry

Check. The leaves are small and usually spiny, but there are different kinds. Some leaves grow in rosettes on dwarf shoots as on page 50, with a bunch of spines or a special leaf under each rosette. There are also long shoots. The small orange-yellow flowers grow in clusters. Their stamens bend in if you can manage to touch the base with a needle. The clusters of small berries may be red, pink, yellow or purple, and round or oval in shape.

✱✱✱ See how many different kinds you can find. They are often called Berberis in parks, and some are evergreen. See if they will grow from seed.

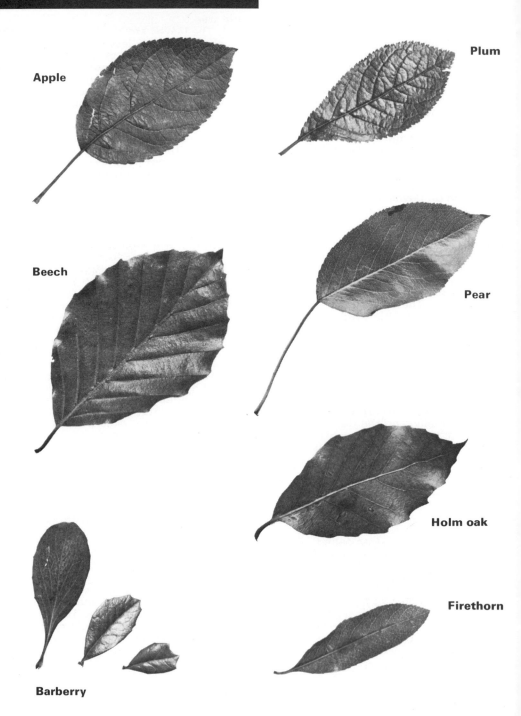

Apple

Plum

Beech

Pear

Holm oak

Barberry

Firethorn

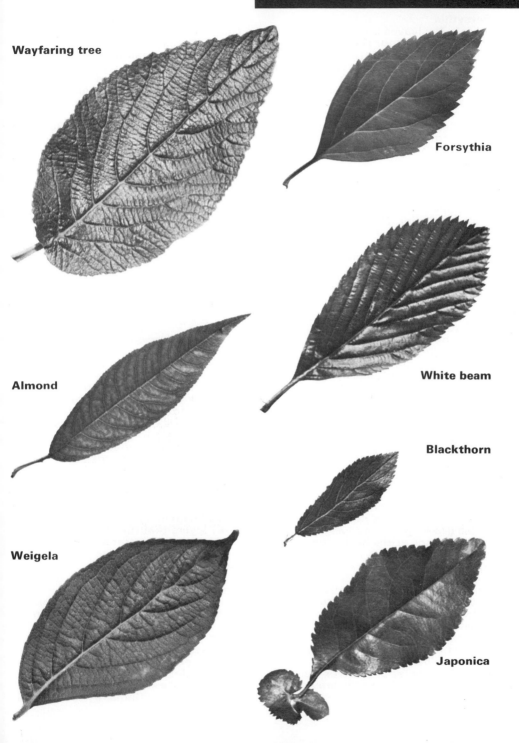

Wayfaring tree

Forsythia

Almond

White beam

Blackthorn

Weigela

Japonica

Forsythia

Check. The leaves are usually only toothed at the top. The yellow, very early flowers have four petals, and come out before the leaves, giving the name Golden Bells to the bush.

*** Look at the parts of the flower and see if fruits are produced. Do you find more flowers on new or old branches? Forsythia plants can be grown from cuttings. Can you guess the origin of the name?

White beam

Check. The leaves are fairly large, with dense white felt underneath, especially when they are young. They are not in pairs. The clusters of small white flowers are followed by red berries. There are several varieties of this small tree, e.g. that on page 78.

*** The autumn colours are often very fine.

Blackthorn

Check. The leaf is small and the dark stalk often has two thin wings at the base. The small black branches often end in spines. The small white flowers usually come out before the leaves, and cover the bush like snow. The fruit is a small, sour, black plum, with a bluish 'bloom', and is called a sloe.

*** Young flowers poke out the stigma before the petals open. There are many suckers that help the bushes spread, and sometimes they cover a big area with impenetrable thicket.

Japonica

Check. This spiny plant can grow as a low bush or be trained against a wall. The shiny leaves are not in pairs, and those growing on long twigs have a pair of wings at the base. The flowers are red, pink or white and open early. The future fruit shows as a green lump underneath.

*** This plant is often called cydonia, chaenomeles, or quince, which is really a related tree. Most people use the name that tells you its original home.
Look at the parts of the flower and try to see bushes with large fruits like apples or the true quince in this picture. The seeds are said to grow easily and the plant also produces suckers.

Wayfaring tree

This is a kind of viburnum.
Check. The paired leaves often have a quilted surface and fluffy stalks. The small white flowers form clusters on the bush in summer, and the berries stand upright, often showing three colours in one bunch: green, red and black.

*** The winter buds are unusual. Is it true that this bush only grows on chalk? Look for other kinds of viburnum (see the index) and see if you think they are much alike.

Almond tree

Check. The leaf is rather shiny and tough, with small sugar glands on the stalk (page 36). The fruits are green furry cases, splitting to let out a woody meshwork that contains the nut.

The pink flowers have very short stalks and open in very early spring, before the leaves. Peach trees have similar leaves and flowers but different fruits. The spindle tree, growing in chalky districts, has leaves of this shape, but growing in pairs. It has pink, four-lobed fruits with orange-covered seeds inside. They are poisonous.

*** Look in the almond flower for the start of the nut, and try to follow its growth. Take apart a nut to see the parts. The bark strips off in thin corky layers that run round the stem, and the lenticels stretch sideways on thicker branches. But on older trees the bark alters completely.

Weigela

Check. The leaves grow in pairs on a bush with branches often falling in an arch and curving in a swan neck shape. The flowers are large pink trumpets, in bunches.

*** The details of the large flowers are very clear. Occasional twigs have leaves in threes. This plant was brought in from China, by the famous Robert Fortune.

Plane

Check. The leaves are not in pairs, and there is a little hollow in the end of every fresh leaf stalk, like a hat. The bark of all but old trees peels off in flakes at the end of summer, leaving yellowish patches underneath, that change to greenish grey. Most trees have round plane-bobs hanging from the branches for most of the year, and the branches of older trees form snaky curves.

In American books this tree is called the sycamore.

*** The different shapes of leaf and the intergrades between them, depend partly on the age of the tree and whether it was pruned recently. Nearly all of them can be found on a full grown tree, but they grow in different places and fall at different times, starting in June. See what you can find and collect. Occasionally you will find a tree with very deep cut leaves, belonging to a different variety. When the spring buds open some of the inner scales form large 'hats' covered with orange fur. In spring, the young leaves are covered with brownish fur and hang down. Each young leaf has a tube at its base, that protects the next leaf till it grows out. These tubes usually fall off when the leaves enlarge, but they sometimes stay on a well-lit shoot and grow a green toothed edge (see photograph of the biggest leaf). The pollen flowers are packed in small round greenish catkins, but higher on the tree there are some seed catkins with bright red stigmas all over. These will form the plane-bobs. They look ripe in autumn but the fruits do not fall off the bobs till next spring. I do not know if they need time, or dry weather or strong winds

to make them fall. Records of weather and time of falling would help. The bobs themselves seem to wear out their stalks. Look for the patterned bob and its tattered stalk in birds nests and on the ground in early spring. Each small fruit has a tuft of fluff that irritates sensitive skins. Does the fluff act like a parachute? In August or very early September, try to follow the colour changes of a piece of bark before and after it falls off. If you wet the bark it will brighten the colours. Find fallen pieces of bark and look for the marks of earlier scaling and for interesting shapes. Trees that have been much injured by penknives will only produce small greyish scales. Try to see how injured places are cast off or form rounded seals, with pleats. The twigs often keep growing the whole summer, so pale young leaves can be seen at almost any time. When growth stops, the whole stem tip, with its protective tube, falls off. Does the plane tree really do better than other trees in towns? It is not attractive to insect-eating birds and we might do better with some different trees. Fertile seed is only produced in good summers.

Flowering currant

Check. This shrub has smallish leaves with hairy stalks and a fruity scent, with hanging clusters of small pink flowers very early in the year.

*** The flowers attract many early bees and may leave a few berries. Some of the bigger bud scales have a little leaf on top.

Plane

Plane

Flowing currant

Sycamore

Norway maple

Field maple

Sycamore

Check. The leaves are paler underneath, and curl tightly as they dry. The leaf stalks vary in length and leaves on long stems can be deeply lobed. Leaves and the greenish buds grow in pairs (page 18). The flowers are in large green hanging catkins, and the winged fruits are in pairs.

*** Some fruits are triple, not double. Are triples as common as one in ten, or less? Page 21 has some

information about the whirling fruits, and page 29 will help if you are taking the fruit apart. When the seedlings grow next spring, they unfold the long seed leaves, so you can recognise them easily. Many will have travelled far from the tree: try to find the furthest. There are many

insects and pests on sycamores, including Tarspot fungus and Nail galls (page 35). The winter buds are green, but can turn red as they open. The bud scales are in a series, and the longest may have a tiny leaf on top. The outermost scale of a winter bud may also have a tiny black leaf on top. The catkins come out after the leaves. They are large, and the separate flowers are easy to see. Bees are attracted by the nectar. In the middle of some flowers you can see the future winged fruit, in miniature, with long stigmas on top. It is easy to collect fallen flowers that show how the fruit grows. Other flowers on the catkin have stamens only. The bark is smooth and silvery for many years, so the scar-seals and branch-wrinkles show up well. In time, however, big flakes of bark peel off. When trees start to fruit, the branches fork a great deal, with a fruit stalk in each angle. We have many foreign kinds of sycamore in Britain now, with leaves of very different shapes and unusual fruits and bark. They are usually called maples, especially in North America. The Sugar maple is tapped for its sugary sap.

Norway maple

Check. The leaves grow in pairs and are about the same colour above and below. The teeth have narrow points with curving arches in between. The flowers open very early in the year, before the leaves, and are bright green, in upright clusters. The fruits are like flat sycamores, with no real bulge for the seed.

*** This tree is closely related to the sycamore. Look at the same points as for sycamore, and compare them. The bark of older trees is different from sycamore, and the leaves can turn bright yellow in autumn. On sunny days in early spring, look for the early bees that are attracted to the flowers. They include mining bees, with reddish tails. When a young leaf is pulled off, a whitish latex comes out and sets to a rubbery lump, perhaps to seal the wound.

Field maple

Check. This tree is also related to the sycamore, but the leaves are smaller and have very rounded lobes. They grow in pairs. The wings of the fruits stick straight out sideways, unlike those of sycamore, which are at about 100 degrees to each other.

*** Look at the same points as for sycamore, and compare them. Look in parks for foreign maples.

Holly

Check. The leaves never grow in pairs. They are shiny, with a strong pale edge that continues into the spines. (Check with Osmanthus and Holm oak.)
∗∗∗ Older trees are said to have fewer spines, especially on flowering branches and high up. Try counting the spines in different places. What use are the spines? (Deer often eat holly leaves.) Look for leaf miners (page 33). The leaves live more than a year, and you can find their age by the girdle scars. In the end they fall, but not in autumn. They make good skeleton leaves (page 19) that you can often find under the bush or in ponds. Old parks and churchyards often have variegated varieties or leaves with extra prickles, or none, or broad, flat, or crumpled, or with yellow

berries. The branches thicken where they join the trunk and there are often clear branch wrinkles and branch seals. The early spring flowers are small and whitish, and they open among the dirty old leaves.
The numbers of petals and stamens varies a little. Some trees have no proper pistils and grow no berries. Others have little or no pollen, but can grow berries. Look for the two kinds and see which grow bigger, and which have more flowers.
The new leaves are beautifully rolled in the bud, for the spines are soft.

Osmanthus

Check. The leaves grow in pairs and are flatter than holly. Those growing high up may lose their spines.
∗∗∗ Look for small scented white flowers late in the year, and nearly black berries. Robert Fortune brought this plant to England.

Snowberry

Check. The older leaves are dark, and most of them have no lobes (see page 51). They grow in pairs. The flowers are tiny pink bells (page 52) on the ends of thin twigs, and are followed by white berries.

Ivy

Check. The leaves are tough, evergreen, sometimes variegated. The plant is a climber but can have quite thick stems. Leaves that grow high up and near flowers are smooth, as on page 50.
∗∗∗ Try to see how ivy climbs, and whether it pierces tree trunks. Look for flowers late in the year. They grow in greenish clusters and are visited by bees in search of the nectar. The green poisonous fruits ripen to black by next year. Small cuttings of ivy can be rooted in pots, as house plants, but layering is usually better.

Grey poplar and near relatives

Check. Leaf stalks growing high up are flattened sideways, at the leaf end, and young leaves have whitish felt underneath. Leaves near the tips of long shoots are lobed, but the rest are more rounded. The small twigs and buds are hairy. White poplar and aspen are not easy to distinguish, for these trees vary, experts disagree, and there is more than one kind of leaf on each tree. If you find a tree with all the leaves lobed, and white felt on all *old* leaves, it is *white* poplar. If the leaves are small and *very* rounded (except on long branches, where some are shaped like birch), and if the twigs and buds have no hairs, the tree is aspen.
∗∗∗ At one stage the bark is whitish, with black diamonds, but this changes with age. Poplar roots spread out and can undermine the foundations of buildings, if they are too near.
The long fluffy catkins are a fine sight in early spring. Some trees have pollen catkins and others have seed catkins. These ripen early, and cover the ground with white fluffy seeds which may grow the same year. Often the fluff has no seeds in it. A few of the twigs are sometimes cast off like oak twigs. The wood, especially aspen wood, is good for matchsticks, as it can hold wax.

∗∗∗ Try to find a leaf series along a branch. Look for suckers that form new plants. Try to see the future berry under the flower, and follow its growth. Do birds like the berries? Will the seeds grow?

73

Ivy

Holly

Osmanthus

Grey poplar

Snowberry

Virginia creeper

Hornbeam

Oak

Virginia creeper
Check. These shiny leaves are not evergreen. The plant climbs with little pads on side branches, and has some smaller narrow leaves, and sometimes a few trefoils.

*** Try to watch a climbing pad fastening itself on, and look for flowers and fruit. Seeds can be bought, and grow quite easily. The autumn colours are brilliant, and old vines have fissured bark.

Hornbeam
This is the winged fruit (see page 21). The real leaf is on page 59.

Oak
Check. The fruits of all oak trees are acorns, with a cup round the base, but sometimes the cup is shaggy. The twigs and branches rarely curve, but stick out stiffly, and may have zig-zags.

*** The twigs have rounded orange-brown buds, not in pairs, but with a cluster at the tip of the stem (page 18). Turkey oak buds are shaggy. Each bud has many scales, arranged regularly, and they show well when the bud is swelling in spring. The pollen catkins are long and hang down. If you let them open indoors, they will give off clouds of pollen at a touch. The pistils are very small, like pin-heads on stalks.

The twigs stop growing early in the year and form 'winter' buds, but in July and August, some of these buds grow out and the tree has a second spring in one year. Of course the new shoots upset the girdle scar count. In late summer and autumn a great many twigs are neatly cut off and fall to the ground. You can recognise these cast twigs by their swollen, clean-cut end. Look at twigs that are still on the tree, to see where the break comes. Oak wood is very tough and resists decay because so much of it is heart wood, containing preservatives. Look at old, worn oak furniture and you will see pale raised streaks of different shapes. These are the hard rays which help you recognise oak. Old oak trees often have dead branches sticking up, and then they are called 'stag-headed'. There are a great many pests, insects and galls on oaks, especially on young trees. Perhaps that is why they need the new shoots in summer. In early spring, for example, there may be hundreds of oak roller caterpillars on one tree, winding themselves up on silk threads if they fall. Look for rolled leaves. They have a caterpillar inside at first, but later the black pupa, from which there comes a small pale green moth. If most of the leaves are eaten, the tree will open new buds straight away. Galls (page 36) are common, and if you keep fallen 'oak apple' galls in summer, some of the tiny wasps will come out quite soon. If you look at young trees, you will see that many of the branches are lost, perhaps by being turned into galls, so that growth is irregular, with zig-zags.

Jays are said to carry away and hide more acorns than other creatures. Watch the trees for birds in autumn. Open an acorn to see the parts (pages 28, 29). Oak trees do not all have the same size of acorn. Collect some and find the tree with the biggest average. Look for a tiny yellow cup-fungus on last years rotting acorns. Collect a

sprouting acorn (page 30) in spring and grow it in a pot or in a special glass acorn-cup. There are many foreign oaks grown in this country, such as the red oak and the cork oak. Most of them come from America or from the Mediterranean region. Look at page 56 for the Holm oak, and see if you can find others in parks and gardens. The leaves vary, but all oaks have acorns when full grown.

Ginkgo

Check. The leaves are thick, with many near-parallel veins. They look much the same on top as underneath. Most of the leaves are clustered on short shoots.

*** This is sometimes called the Maidenhair tree. Look at a Maidenhair Fern and see what you think of this name. The dwarf shoots and opening buds are interesting. Look for pollen catkins in spring. There are also a few trees in this country which have tiny lumps on the end of special stalks. These will grow into big seeds, with a juicy outer coat, but they are never inside a pistil or a fruit. The ginkgo grew in very ancient times.

You can read about fossil ginkgos, about their present-day home, and how they were brought to this country.

Guelder rose and Snowball tree

Check. This is really a kind of viburnum, not a rose. There are small sugar glands (page 36) on the leaf stalk, and on the wings at the base of the leaf. Cultivated kinds may have round bunches of white flowers (Snowball trees), but wild plants have a flat plate of very tiny flowers, with larger ones only round the edge.

*** Compare this plant with a real rose. See which of the two kinds of flowers produce red berries and read how new plants can be grown if no berries are found.

Tulip tree

Check. No other tree has a leaf with this big notch and tiny spike to the midrib. It is really a kind of Magnolia, not a tulip.

*** The flower is shaped like a tulip but is green with orange patches. It has many long stamens and, in the centre, a bunch of flat leaf-like pistils, each with a stigma at the top (like Magnolia, page 53).

Compare it with a tulip. The buds have an unusual shape and are worth watching as they open. The bark is furrowed and later breaks into a mosaic. Read how Tulip trees came to this country, and where from. Fossil Magnolias first grew in very ancient times, when the animals were quite different from today.

White beam

Check. There are several different kinds, with slightly different leaves, (e.g. that on page 67) but all have grey felt underneath, especially when they are young. There are clusters of small white flowers and then red or orange berries. The various kinds of Service tree can be very similar in the leaves, but the fruits are different.

*** The opening buds and autumn colours are particularly worth seeing.

Hawthorn

Check. Some of the stems end in thorns. The clustered flowers are usually white, with red stamens and a strong scent. There is also a red cultivated kind, and a double variety. The fruits are small red 'haws', in bunches, each with a ring of sepals at the tip. The leaves are very varied, and some are much more deeply lobed than others.

*** Most of the leaves are in clusters on short shoots, but there are also longer branches, with the leaves spaced out. The leaves on these long branches have big, well-shaped wings at the base. Each twig has a changing series of leaf-shapes, starting from small simple ones, and the series is different for long shoots, short shoots and flowering shoots. Look out for varieties with deep lobes. Try to trace the growth from flower to fruit, and find whether many of the flowers form fruits. Various insects can be found, feeding on the leaves, and a special, small grey toadstool, with light brown spores, grows on old, fallen fruits. Seedlings often grow well. See if you can find any that have travelled a long way from the parent bush. The bark of the old trees makes a mosaic.

Tulip tree

Ginkgo

White beam

Guelder rose

Hawthorn

Index

a

acacia (False)   40
ailanthus   40
alder   60
almond   68
ants   36
aphids   36
apple (crab)   65
araucaria   48
art   4
ash   41
Ash-leaved maple   44
aspen   73
aucuba   64
azalea   52

b

bamboo   48
barberry   50 65
   Holly-leaved   41
Bay laurel   56
beech   52 66
berberis   50 65
big leaves   7
birch   57
Bird cherry   61
blackberry   44
Black mulberry   57
Black poplar   57
blackthorn   68
Bladder senna   40
books   31
box   56
bramble   44
broom   37 47
Buddleia   61
buds   18
Butterfly flower (Buddleia)   61

c

Canadian redwood   48
catalpa   49
cedar   46
cellulose   18
Chaenomeles   68
cherry   61
Cherry bay (Cherry laurel)   64
Cherry laurel   64
chestnut (Sweet)   61
clematis   44
collections   4 10
colour   13 16
conker   30 37
cotoneaster   56
crab   65
Cricket Bat willow   61
cupressus (cypress)   45
currant (flowering)   69
cut-leaved maple   37
cydonia   68
cypress   45

d

damaged leaves   34 35
Daphne   52
decay   19
d'Incarville   40
dinosaurs   53 77
dogwood   52

e

elder   41
elm   49 60
euonymus (spindle)   64
evergreens   17
Evergreen spindle (euonymus)
   64

f

False acacia   40
field maple   72
fir   48
firethorn   65
Flowering currant   69
fluffy fruits   23
food   30
Forsythia   68
Fortune   53
fruits   20
fungus   36
fungus roots   52

g

galls   36
ginkgo   77
Golden Bells   68
Grey poplar   73
Guelder rose   77

h

haws   77
hawthorn   77
hazel   66
hips   44
histogram   11
holly   54 73
Holly-leaved barberry   41
Holm oak   56 66
honeysuckle   56
hornbeam   60 74
horsechestnut   37

i

ivy   49 73

j

Japanese maple   37
Japanese spindle   64
Japonica   68
juicy fruits   24

l

laburnum   37
lammas shoots   76
larch   45
laurel
   aucuba   64
   Bay   56
   Cherry   64
   Portugal   64
Laurustinus   56
   (viburnum)
leaf
   damage   33
   eaters   33
   and leaflet   32
   miners   33
   rollers   33
   rubbings   5
   scars   17
   sizes   10
   stalks   17
   stencils   6 7
lilac   49
lime   49 57
locust   40
Lombardy poplar   57
long-leaved willow   61

m

Magnolia   53 77
maidenhair tree   77
maple
   Ash-leaved   44
   Cut-leaved   37
   Field   72
   Japanese   37
   Norway   72
maps   11 12
mast (beech)   28
mast years   28
mildew   36
mistletoe   48
Mock orange   57
models   12
Monkey Puzzle   48
mulberry   57

n

native trees   33
Norway spruce   33 48
   maple   72
nuts   28 29

o

oak   75
   Holm   56 66
orange (blossom)   57
Osmanthus   73

p

peach   68
pear   51 65
philadelphus   57
pine   45
plane   69
plaster casts   9
plum   65
poplar
    Black   57
    Grey   73
    Lombardy   57
    White   73
Portugal laurel   64
prints   7 8
privet   53
Pussy willow   56
pyracantha   65

q

quince   68
    (Japonica)

r

rhododendron   53
Robinia   40
rolled leaves   33
rose   44
rowan   40
rubbings   5

s

sallow   56
Scots pine   45
seeds   29 30
Service tree   77
shadow leaves   53
Short-leaved willow   56
Silver fir   48
skeleton leaves   53
skimmia   56
sloe   68
Snowball tree   77
snowberry   51 73
sorting   4
Spanish broom   47
spindle   64
spruce   48
stencils   6   7
sugar glands   36
sumach   40
Sweet bay   56
    chestnut   61
sycamore   72
syringa   57
syringa (lilac)   49

t

tamarisk   46
tarspot   36
thuja   45
toadstools   52 77
Tradescant   33
Traveller's Joy   44

Tree of Heaven   40
Tulip tree   77
Turkey oak   75

v

veins   6
viburnum   56
    Guelder rose   77
    Wayfaring tree   68
Virginia creeper   37 75
vitamin C   44

w

walnut   44
Wayfaring tree   68
Weigela   68
Western 'hemlock'   48
Western red 'cedar' (thuja)   45
White
    beam   77
    birch   57
    poplar   73
willow Long-leaved   61
    Short-leaved   56
winged fruits   21
Wisteria   41
Wych elm   60

y

yew   48

LONGMAN GROUP LIMITED
Longman House,
Burnt Mill, Harlow, Essex CM20 2JE, England
and Associated Companies throughout the World.

First published 1969
Fifth impression 1983
ISBN 0 582 18162 3

Printed in Hong Kong by Wilture Printing Co Ltd